Journal of the Plague Year

To Nuria,

Best wishes.

Max.

Journal of the Plague Year

Max Stafford-Clark

NICK HERN BOOKS
London
www.nickhernbooks.co.uk

A NICK HERN BOOK

Journal of the Plague Year
first published in Great Britain in 2014
by Nick Hern Books Limited, The Glasshouse,
49a Goldhawk Road, London W12 8QP

Cover art by Martin Rowson
Author photo by John Haynes

Designed and typeset by Nick Hern Books
Printed and bound in Great Britain by
Ashford Colour Press Ltd, Gosport, Hampshire

A CIP catalogue record for this book is available
from the British Library

ISBN 978 1 84842 179 0

To Stella, to Kitty and to Mai

Contents

Preface

Perhaps I must begin with a bit of an apology, not least to Daniel Defoe and to you, dear reader; *Journal of the Plague Year* is not really a journal, and it covers rather more than one year. It contains elements of memoir and autobiography, but it is principally a howl of rage at Arts Council England's round of cuts announced in March 2011. Despite claims from the highest levels of the Arts Council (Liz Forgan, Chair at the time) that this was an 'open and fair process' determined by 'just and clear principles', I believed then and still believe that this was an ill-considered and panicky move by a timid Arts Council who, at the behest of a bullying Coalition government harrumphing about austerity and the need for every sector of the welfare state to take a hit, simply cut as much as they could from every arts organisation that would nonetheless survive.

This book could equally well be called 'Two Christmases and an Easter', since those were the only occasions I had time to undertake a sustained period of writing. I work with writers on a daily basis; I'm married to one, but it was chastening to discover at first hand that Time to Think is even more vital than Time to Write. I started to write over Christmas 2011 and then picked up the manuscript again at Christmas 2012. I had then accumulated enough material to send to my indomitable editor, Nick Hern. He pointed out that I was attempting to write three books at once and suggested that one would be quite enough. I started again using the existing material as a quarry and completed it at Easter 2013. My heartfelt thanks to Nick Hern; to Barney Norris, my PA, who corrected my spelling while we argued about the use of the apostrophe; to my wife, Stella Feehily, for reading endless drafts at all times of the day and night; and to my mother-in-law, Mai Feehily, whose living room I hogged over Christmas 2012 while taking advantage of her generous and splendid hospitality. I must also thank Polly Teale, Michael Attenborough, Ian Redford, John Hollingworth and Karen Hayes from whose correspondance I quote. Nor should I forget Frank Endwright, Out of Joint's Relationship Manager at Arts Council England, who has endured an amount of slings and arrows with remarkable equanimity and friendliness. Long may The Relationship continue. To all, great thanks.

*

Arts Council England retain the copyright in all emails by their employees quoted in this book.

Journal of the Plague Year

On 30th March 2011, Arts Council England announced a round of funding cuts that were to have a deep and long-lasting effect on a number of theatre companies—my own company, Out of Joint, among them. We were shocked and dismayed to learn that our annual funding would be reduced by over £99,432.[1] In other words, we were to lose 20% of our total funding. As I write, we are still struggling to put together a programme that minimises these traumatic effects.

Everyone knew hard times were coming to the theatre. The country was in an economic crisis and cuts in theatre grants had been widely predicted. The Conservative economic line at the time—that austerity was the way out of recession and that spending should be reduced across the board—had its most profound effects on welfare, healthcare, housing and the pillars of our society, but the arts were to be slashed as well. Arguments that the theatre industry as a whole made a net profit for the UK fell on deaf ears—it was to be hair shirts and pinched pennies all round. My wife, Stella Feehily, is writing a play about the NHS, and while researching the project we met Ken Clarke, former Conservative Minister for Health. He is the worst kind of Tory: personable, witty, charming and rather wise. At the end of our meeting we were chatting casually and I asked him

---

1. Together with the 10% cut suffered by all institutions the previous year, the total loss amounted to nearly £130,000.

what was going to happen to the theatre: 'You're going to be cut,' he said with a huge grin. 'Yes, you're certainly going to be cut.'

Nevertheless, it was a huge shock to learn the scale of the cut imposed on Out of Joint. My own experience of Thatcher's proposed cuts at the beginning of the eighties had taught me how rash it was to take state funding for granted, but Out of Joint had been sustained and supported by Arts Council England (ACE) for eighteen years. Our relationship with them had been the bedrock of all our artistic success, and now that relationship was thrown off-balance. There had been no sign or signal in any way that we had incurred their displeasure. Nor was there any immediate explanation forthcoming as to why we had been singled out for a cut. There was just a new financial reality in which our established production model, touring two new plays each year as widely as possible around the UK, was suddenly imperilled. This book is an attempt to come to terms with their decision, and to tell the story of our first hesitant steps into the perilous new world the Arts Council had defined.

At the time of the announcement, Out of Joint had an Arts Council grant of £525,000, and our turnover was just over £1,000,000 annually. In common with most other companies, including the National Theatre, Arts Council funding made up about 45% of our turnover. This compares with 70% or 75% for equivalent companies in Germany, France or Holland, but was, on the other hand, considerably more than the 10% in Federal funding which our colleagues in the United States could expect, while in Australia state funding can be as little as 7.5% of turnover. Our previous relationship with the Arts Council had been a harmonious and, I thought, mutually satisfactory one. We took new work to the regions, touring from ten to twenty-four weeks a year, playing in major cities such as Liverpool and Leeds as well as smaller county towns like Bury St Edmunds, Bolton and Salisbury. Mark Long of *The People Show* once said to me, 'We're a 60 people a night outfit—wherever we play, we get 60 people a night.' By the same anecdotal criteria, I reckoned Out of Joint was a 200 people per night outfit. Sometimes we soared to 400 or even 500, and occasionally we dropped to under 100, but regional audiences had been built up consistently, or so I thought. But there was some evidence that regional audiences had peaked around 2005 and were becoming more wary and more circumspect in their theatrical choices. Price too was an increasing factor towards the end of the noughties—audiences began to peak in terms of numbers on a Tuesday or a Wednesday, when ticket offers were at their most plentiful, and thin out at the end of the week when concessions were not generally available. Of course, we had no control over the pricing policies of our host theatres; they determined their own ticket policies, but it had become clear that price resistance was growing. Out of Joint had had the odd *succès fou*—*Shopping and Fucking*, *The Permanent Way*, *Feelgood*—and several *succès d'estime*—*Macbeth*, *The Big Fellah*, *Duck* and *A State Affair* among them. We understood we were providing new work of a particular calibre and taste that was not covered by any other company. The work followed no specific political agenda but had a purposeful and inquisitive curiosity that poked into the unregarded corners of English life and society. Such plays as *The Permanent Way*, *A State Affair* and *The Big Fellah* depicted issues, lives and obsessions that were new to the stage. I had been lucky to have had a career during a period when the theatre was the medium for social debate and the medium through which we examined our history. Of course, this has not always been the case. Walpole's Licensing Act of 1737 introduced the authority of the Lord Chamberlain as censor and effectively exiled the theatre from its native hinterland of sex and politics for over two hundred years. While in Australia, the novel is the medium of social examination—*The Great World* (David Malouf), *The Secret River* and *The Lieutenant* (Kate Grenville), *Out of Ireland* (Christopher Koch) and indeed *The Playmaker* (Thomas Keneally) are all great novels that give Australians back their history—in England, the theatre continues to do that job.

All that we had achieved at Out of Joint was threatened by the cut. Graham Cowley, Out of Joint's producer and my friend and colleague of forty years, responded to the new financial situation by slashing administrative costs wherever money could be saved, but we have never been a profligate organisation, and it was immediately clear that the foremost impact of our reduced funding would be a concomitant reduction in production capacity. With spending stripped back across the organisation, the only way to absorb the remaining reduction in income was to reduce the number of touring weeks; the number of weeks we employed actors and technical staff; the number of actors in our plays; even the number of plays we produced annually; or alternatively to programme work that appealed to a larger audience. The grim truth was that a reduction of 25% in fact threatened to halve our production output.

My first inclination in the wake of our own bad news was to try to humanise the faceless institution of the Arts Council and discover why Out of Joint had been singled out for a cut of such brutality that it threatened our continued existence. Graham Cowley and I sought an immediate meeting with Frank Endwright, our 'Relationship Manager', and George Darling, the Director of Drama for London. In answer to our questions at that meeting, much emphasis was placed on the high 'subsidy per seat' costs that Out of Joint incurred, and Darling actually said that other 'providers' could supply the Arts Council with new work at less cost. In other words, Out of Joint wasn't cost efficient. We took this news back to our office in Finsbury Park, determined first to address our business model and see what savings could be made to ensure the company was able to keep producing, and secondly to illustrate why our work cost what it did and why we desperately needed the money that had been cut.

We had been and continued to be engaged in that most difficult and arcane of sciences, the discovery and development of new writers and new plays, and taking them beyond the metropolitan audiences of the London 'new writing' theatre scene to reach a national audience. Neither of these objectives can be achieved cheaply or easily, and we resolved to defend and underline our achievements as well as to find a way of continuing our work with decreased support. Many of the plays we produced needed time for research and development in workshop mode—this investment, the provision of time for the development and rehearsal of plays for which I have campaigned throughout my career, was a cornerstone of our work, and could not be stripped away without imperilling the creation of plays themselves. And although we had been successful in getting help for this vital aspect of our work from the National Theatre Studio and from other varied sources, it still made us expensive. In fact, in the course of 2012/13 we received help from the RSC, Bristol Old Vic, the National Theatre of Wales, the University of Hertfordshire, Bridgend College and LAMDA, as well as the National Theatre Studio. Although facilities and other help amounted to many thousands of pounds, it was, alas, not represented in our balance sheets as 'fundraising', as it did not pass through our accounts, and was therefore disregarded by the Arts Council when they made their crucial decision.

Both for Graham and for me it was important to establish the grounds for the cut. I wondered whether it had anything to do with age. An earlier assessment from the Arts Council had made some mention of the board needing to address the 'problem' of replacing the founder members of the company (Graham and me). Did the Arts Council think I was past my sell-by date? Were they endeavouring to make me fall on my sword and embrace one of the dreaded 'R' words? Resignation? Retirement? Indeed, they had imposed a form of Relegation, but we were bent upon Rebuttal, Resistence, Rejuvenation and Resurgence.

*

As well as being several years past national retirement age, I had suffered a major stroke in 2006 which had hospitalised me for six months. I got out of hospital in December 2006 and joyfully returned to the rehearsal room in January 2007. But, alas, it was too early and I wasn't really very good. I would watch a runthrough of Alistair Beaton's play, *King of Hearts*, with my co-director Ramin Gray, and see at once that it wasn't particularly good, but could find no words to help or improve it. My analysis was in place but my imagination seemed sadly absent. Things got better in April 2007 when I directed a 'Long Project' with an excellent group of young actors at LAMDA. This was to become *Mixed Up North* a year later and marked a substantial step on my road to recovery (another 'R' word).

Why was I not a particularly good director of *King of Hearts*? What is a bad director? I believe the answer to these questions is quite simple: a good director is one who is able to help the actors to their characters and to their performances. I had (temporarily, thank God) lost this ability, and so I was a Not-Very-Good-At-All Director. For the first professional play that I directed at the Edinburgh Traverse in 1966, I hadn't been very good either. But that was largely inexperience. My first steps in directing were conducted by Susan Williamson, an actress in that play to whom I will be eternally grateful. I wasn't very good, but I did have a beautiful MG TD, and I used to give Susan a lift back to her digs every night after rehearsal. In return, she would give me a fifteen-minute seminar on the basic points of direction: 'If you want George to grow a moustache in that part then he has to start now'; 'If you want Heather to dominate that scene you must get her out from behind the desk'; 'If you want me to look really relaxed in the sofa scene I could put my feet up on the chair, but then I would have to be wearing trousers not a skirt.' Above all she taught me the most fundamental lesson for a young director—which was, Don't Be Scared of the Actors. Of course they know more than you, but they are a repository of wisdom and experience on which you can draw.

One of the best definitions of a director's function came from my daughter, Kitty, when she was five years old. I used to drive her to nursery school every morning, and we would regularly do an improvisation together. On some occasions we would be an ambulance team, or I would be a train driver or policeman. On this particular occasion the role I was allocated was that of taxi driver. We had recently been on a journey with a female driver, and in a fit of inspiration Kitty insisted, 'Be a lady taxi driver!' Doing my best in my new role, I enquired why her parents weren't available to take her to school. 'Oh, they are in theat,' said Kitty, as if this covered all laxness. 'Are they actors?' the taxi driver enquired. 'Yes, actors,' said Kitty firmly. 'Really... your dad is an actor, is he?' I countered. Kitty wavered. 'Well no, he's the watcher,' she said. And that indeed is the major part of the role.

I am a cripple these days. We rather shrink from the 'C' word and prefer to say Disabled or 'Person With Limited Mobility', but I think often of my old friend, Ian Dury, who wrote the lyrics for four or five plays I directed in the late eighties, most notably *A Jovial Crew* at Stratford and *Serious Money* by Caryl Churchill. He was a hugely influential and original lyricist and had had a number-one hit with 'Hit Me With Your Rhythm Stick'. He had had polio as a child and walked with a stick and a metal brace on one leg. He was a charismatic and fascinating companion until he'd had a few drinks— which, let's face it, was every night—when he could turn feral. I recall one night in the Royal Court bar when he'd had a few. He whacked his metal calliper with his stick and said, 'Do you know how often I think about this, mate? Every fucking morning, every fucking morning.' So do I. Ian wasn't reticent about his disability; a year earlier at Stratford with the RSC we had been rehearsing one Saturday morning. We had to stop at one o'clock to release actors who were in matinees that afternoon. After eight Saturday morning cups of coffee I was bursting for a pee, but the buses had already arrived full of matinee-goers and there was long queue. Ian passed me in the corridor. 'You want to try the Raspberries', mate,' he said. 'You meet a better class of person,' and he gestured towards the disabled toilet. Twenty minutes later we were sitting outside The Dirty Duck enjoying the first pint of the weekend. 'Raspberries?' I enquired. 'Of course,' he said, 'Raspberry ripple, cripple.' Since Ian's death in 2000 and my stroke in 2006, Stella and I have been to more raspberry toilets than I care to remember. The National Theatre's are the best whilst the Lyric Hammersmith's need more regular attention, and non-disabled people trespass infuriatingly in the Royal Court's, just as I had at Stratford.

For the first six months after I came out of hospital I travelled train-wise by wheelchair. GNER and South West Trains were very attentive, and First Great Western were usually very good. But there was one occasion when we arrived at an unmanned and unlit Thatcham station on a February evening to pick up my car. Stella and I stared disconcerted at the drop onto the platform as the electric doors slid open. We could do nothing, and would have departed helplessly squeaking to Newbury, Swindon and Points West had two hefty commuters not sprung to their feet, lifted up the wheelchair and swung it out onto the platform. 'Be lucky, mate,' said one as the doors slid shut. I can't say it's a huge compensation, but we raspberries do often bring out the best in people. Stella and I went to Cuba as part of the charismatic Elyse Dodgson's mission to convert the world to 'Royal Courtism'. The system of theatre in Cuba is essentially based on a Soviet model, where the director is auteur supreme. Her revolutionary work was to encourage the writer and director to work together. It would be fair to say that this was unprecedented in Cuban practice. Cuba is very fifties, not a ramp or disabled access anywhere, but whenever Stella and I approached a curb a burly brown arm from a passer-by or a fellow tourist would descend to assist us onto the pavement.

Since I came out of hospital at the end of 2006, I have had very vivid dreams. Three or four nights ago I dreamt I had mislaid my stick on the top of a bus, but hey presto, I could walk fine and didn't need it. I often have driving dreams where I am driving any one of the variety of delicious cars I have owned over the years, from the 1932 Austin 7 once owned by my father Max, given to me on my seventeenth birthday, to the lovely Jensen Interceptor I owned for five years in the early nineties. In one particularly vivid dream I was playing rugby for an England Under-21 XV at Twickenham. I awoke covered in sweat remembering every move and every pass. I played rugby seriously as a young man but never reached the exalted heights of my dream. When I woke my first concern was that the sheets would be covered with mud. But the most curious aspect was that I remained myself. I had had a stroke and limped clumsily from line-out to scrum and experienced some difficulty passing one-handed. Even in the dream I thought it curious that the poor England selectors were so desperate that they had had to select a sixty-six-year-old stroke victim for their Under-21 XV.

The stroke had happened on 12th July 2006. Stella and I were driving back from Stratford-upon-Avon, where we had stayed the night after seeing a performance of *Henry IV, Part 1*, and receiving an honorary doctorate from Warwick University. We stopped off at Lodge Farm and had lunch with my uncle in a local pub in Western Turville. I had whitebait. I drove back to Out of Joint's offices in Holloway, parking my lovely Bentley 8 in the underground car park beneath our flat. Not only was this the last time I drove the Bentley, it was to be the last time I would ever drive a car of any kind. Stella went home and I worked in the office until after 6:30 p.m., and then walked uneventfully home. My knee hurt a bit; I had twisted it the week before jumping off a bus (the last time I have ever been on a bus too). When I got home I pressed the numbers into the keypad at the door, but I must have got a digit wrong as it refused to open. Fortunately, somebody else returning after work released the door and let me in. On the top step I stumbled and fell. No bother. I got up, but halfway down a perfectly straight and level corridor I fell again, but this time I was completely unable to get up. I lay on the floor squeaking ineffectually for about five minutes before the porter and a lovely neighbour, Justine, picked me up and walked me the remaining ten yards to the door. Stella said straight away, 'You've had a stroke.' Apparently the left side of my face had dropped. I didn't believe it and said I was simply desperate for a pee. This seemed a low priority to Stella and Justine, who phoned for an ambulance. It took fifty-five minutes to arrive, during which time apparently I chatted incoherently and inconsequentially, still unaware of what had happened. I don't recall the ambulance arriving, but I do remember the lights flashing as we arrived at the Whittington Hospital, which was to be my home for the next three months. After a short wait I was examined by a young man I remember only as Dr Ben. He seemed about fifteen. Two months later, returning in the wheelchair with Stella one afternoon from our regular trip up Whittington Hill to Waterlow Park, we ran into Dr Ben again at the entrance to A and E. 'How are you?' he said. I think I must have replied fairly gloomily. After all, at this point I could only hobble on a Zimmer frame. I had lost the use of my left arm, and the nerves to my eyes had suffered such damage that my left peripheral vision had gone completely. 'Well, at least you're alive,' replied Dr Ben cheerfully; 'we weren't sure there for a while.'

The medical team had diagnosed—and told me the next day—that I had indeed suffered a major stroke, but it took me a long time to grasp quite what that meant. I couldn't walk, but I would often forget this important point, lunge a step or two and fall over, on one occasion nearly knocking myself unconscious as I fell against the toilet pedestal in the bathroom. Five months later, as my time for discharge came nearer, I asked Dr Playford, the formidable senior consultant neurologist at the National Hospital, Queen Square, where I had subsequently been admitted for rehabilitation, whether I could see the CAT scan that had been taken five months previously at the Whittington. 'I don't see why not,' she replied, and the next day a beautiful young man, blond as an angel, and with the accent of a Bondi surfer, sat at the end of my bed with a large foolscap envelope of photos. Most of the NHS staff at the blunt end are a) very young and b) very foreign. He asked how I was, and once again I must have replied fairly negatively. After all, although I could now stagger without the Zimmer frame I could still only hobble. 'Well, mate,' replied my new Australian friend pulling the photos from their large envelope, 'most people who have been through this, you would be attending their memorial service at this point.' The photos depicted what appeared to be an area of scrub at the edge of the Kalahari Desert. It was my brain. However, somebody appeared to

have taken a flame-thrower and scorched a twenty-five-yard-square
area of scrub absolutely flat. It was burned and black. 'You didn't
have one stroke, mate,' continued the surfer, 'I think you had four in
quick succession; they set each other off like Roman candles at a fire-
works party. See, there was one here at the front, one here and two
back here.' His finger traced some particularly blackened areas at the
edge of the Kalahari which had been suffused with blood.

Hospital was like being back at school. The routine, the food—
even the daily physiotherapy was a kind of PT class. Actually, I had
my own way round the food. I had been living with Stella for two
years, so I suppose I had the status of long-term boyfriend, though
we weren't to marry till 2010. But suddenly I found I had acquired
a fairy mother-in-law, if not a fairy godmother. Mai Feehily came
over from Ireland to stay in our flat in Holloway and twice a day in
the middle of a heatwave ferried meals up the steep hill to the Whittington. I had difficulty swallowing and poor Mai traipsed all over
Holloway and Islington to find organic butterscotch ice cream—
which was all I could eat. After a month people in Bundoran, Mai's
home town, began to talk. Why was Mai away from her husband for
so long? For the first three weeks Stella slept in a chair at the bottom of the bed, and thereafter the saddest moment each day was
seeing Stella's shadow in the doorway getting shorter and shorter.
Every morning she was back at 8 a.m. I longed for that moment and
would be awake at six yearning for her arrival.

Damage to the nerves had impaired my sight, and probably my
biggest deficit was that I had lost my left-sided peripheral vision,
which made reading difficult. I regularly missed words on the left-
hand side of the page: an imaginative theatre company called InterAct
came to my rescue. They provide a reading service for long-term
patients, but even so I was astonished one morning to surface from
a doze to find a distinguished-looking woman sitting in an armchair
at the end of my bed reading to me. She read with the fluting, highly
enunciated vowels of somebody who has served a long-term sentence
with the RSC. It was Sara Kestelman, and I was the beneficiary of

her excellent rendition of George Eliot. On the second occasion I had a young woman who had just left drama school. She took one look at me and said, 'So it is you. When I saw your name I wondered if I had time to go home and brush up my audition speeches.' I was delighted to see her. My old friend and co-founder of Joint Stock Theatre, Bill Gaskill, had brought me a new John Updike novel, *Terrorist*. I was enjoying it but my left-sided deficit made progress slow. I happily handed the book over and showed her the place I had reached. She read on, but unknown to both of us the next ten pages contained a vivid description of oral sex between the two protagonists. It would be uncharitable to say that she brought a high level of expertise to the reading, but she certainly read with a level of bravado. At the end she said, 'Well, that's the strangest audition I've ever had.'

InterAct also provided a weekly quiz for patients. One week there was a glitch and a young woman turned up with exactly the same quiz we had had the week before. The turnover of patients and staff happened to have been considerable that week, so my 100% was enormously impressive to both my fellow patients and the medical team who were in attendance. At least it proved that my short-term memory had not been badly impaired, and that my innate capacity for cheating and an irrepressible desire to win were both firmly in place.

On 6th December 2006 I was discharged from the National Hospital, Queen Square, and spent Christmas at home. It wasn't the end of my problems, and in no way was I miraculously healed, but I was enormously relieved to be out of hospital.

A lot of friends knew I had been in hospital and, if they were shocked at my limp and enfeebled left hand, successfully disguised their feelings. However, occasionally I would meet somebody who hadn't heard; one of these was Stephen Frears, who accosted me candidly, saying, 'Good God, what has happened to you?' Stephen and I had watched the 1966 World Cup Final together in Edinburgh in my early days at the Traverse. I remained blissfully unaware of my own appearance. Two years later, after Christmas 2008, I was walking up Parkhurst Road to the Arts Centre opposite Holloway Prison where we were rehearsing. It was uphill and a new route for me, so I think I was making heavy weather of it following too many mince pies. I was wearing trackies and my second-best Armani jacket, as appropriate for rehearsing in a church hall, when we were approached by an obviously homeless man. Instead of asking for money, he held out his hand and offered me a pound coin. I demurred, but he insisted. 'No, go on, get yourself a cup of tea, son. Happy Christmas.' I hadn't thought I looked that bad!

*

I now think my suspicions of ageism on the part of the Arts Council were more than a little paranoid, but on the other hand the Council themselves had done much to justify a degree of suspicion. At a later meeting, in May 2012, George Darling, then Head of Theatre in London, admitted the obvious: that the cuts were pragmatic and imposed on the Arts Council by the Coalition administration. They cut as much as they could wherever they could. The criterion was not how much each company needed, but what was the minimum amount with which a company could survive. In this context, Out of Joint's reserves of over £400,000, accrued over the years as the fruits of various transfers to the West End and Broadway, were suddenly a dangerous thing. Our past successes imperilled our future.

Another thing we took away from our meeting with Endwright and Darling was the possibility of further funding from the Arts Council if touring to 'cold spots' was undertaken. This had come down from Moira Sinclair, head of the Arts Council in London, at a public meeting. I understood a 'cold spot' to be a town at some distance from a regular repertory theatre. This seemed like a policy that had been tailor-made for Out of Joint. We have always toured our work widely round the country, sometimes playing non-theatre venues in order to reach particular audiences, or to set our plays in a particularly apposite light. Our 2010 production of *Mixed Up North* by Robin Soans, for example, had played in several halls, clubs and schools around the Burnley area, where the piece was set, in order to connect with people close to the world of the play. Out of Joint's lasting commitment to an intrepid touring itinerary made me hope this could be a fruitful source of funding. With the help of the University of Hertfordshire, I compiled a list of halls and theatres in the Hatfield/Hertford area where we hoped to tour a play about the last witch trial in England that we were developing with Rebecca Lenkiewicz. This trial had taken place in Hertford itself.

At the same time as we began this longer-term planning, Graham and I realised the quickest and most reliable way of decreasing our 'subsidy per seat' in the immediate future was to revisit the back catalogue—so a production of Caryl Churchill's *Top Girls,* co-produced with the Chichester Festival Theatre, was scheduled for 2011, and this was immediately followed by a revival of Timberlake Wertenbaker's *Our Country's Good* with the Bolton Octagon in 2012. The plan worked, economically: our subsidy per seat went down from £24.56 in 2010/11 to £10.01 in 2011/12 and was maintained at £13.77 in 2012/13. But it also meant that in 2012/13, for the first time in its nineteen-year history, Out of Joint did not produce a new play. To meet the Arts Council's priorities, we were forced to set aside our own. The sad product of the determination of the Arts Council, ushered in by the current Conservative/Lib-Dem government, to measure artistic success by economic criteria, was that the core activities of Out of Joint and many other companies were constrained or curtailed to meet new imperatives.

In June, Frank Endwright, our Relationship Manager, responded to my invitation and came to an early rehearsal of *Top Girls*. He wrote to me afterwards, launching a correspondence that was to become a dominant feature of the next year for me, and which I have threaded through the course of this book in order to best tell our story, as it offers a window into the new pressures that have been placed on us.

8th June 2011

Dear Max,

Thank you for letting me sit in your rehearsals yesterday. It is a wonderfully rich play and the production seems to be cooking very nicely!

In terms of 'cold spots' – we're still developing a strategy around this; including a meaningful definition of a cold spot – this will be related to surveys that look at arts engagement in different communities. It is certainly interesting to see the work you are currently doing. My understanding is that we will have some clear guidance in terms of what we might look for with companies engaging in those cold spots later this year. At that point I think your information will become particularly useful.

I eagerly pursued the 'meaningful definition' Endwright had promised as the project developed:

18th June 2011

Dear Frank,

Ever eager to keep Out of Joint's relationship with our Relationship Manager warm and cosy, I am writing again to badger you about 'cold spots'. The University of Hertfordshire, our co-producers, have raised sufficient money for a development workshop on the 'Witches Project', to be written by Rebecca Lenkiewicz. Prognostications are difficult over the summer vacation, but it seems that next February is a time when our tame academic will be free. [In fact we had two such associates: Stephanie Grainger, whom I had worked with over many years as a Visiting Professor at Hertfordshire, the instigator and driving force behind the workshop I write of here; and Owen Davies, an expert in the history of European witchcraft, whose contribution to the project was to prove invaluable.] So we are eager for your advice on the list of cold spots in Hertfordshire that we have compiled, which are attached with my last email.

Thank you for your help, and looking forward to your response to my previous letter.

Such responses from the Arts Council were hard to come by. Just as their decision-making process at the time of the cuts had been shrouded in secrecy, so their opinion on anything at all that I asked them was difficult to pin down. Frank Endwright, of course, had a party line to toe—though the Arts Council always deny having one, you discover the moment you're kicked the other side of it that there has always been a party line—but gnomic evasion isn't much use when you're fighting to save a company you've spent eighteen years building up. So I remained persistent.

In June 2011 I absented myself from Out of Joint's North London base to direct the Out of Joint production of *Top Girls* at the Chichester Festival Theatre. It was a happy time: Stella and I were lodged in a cottage overlooking the picturesque estuary at Bosham; rehearsal conditions were excellent; the cast were terrific, and the play opened to ecstatic notices. Some of the corduroyed denizens of Chichester were bemused by Caryl's inventive structure and daunted by the surreal dinner party that begins the play. 'It's just a load of drunken women chatting,' I overheard one punter expostulating. Things were easier and audiences were reassured once the London critics had come down and given their approval. I kept Frank in touch with developments.

5th July 2011

Dear Frank,

I got back from Chichester yesterday, and the first thing I have done is to review the correspondence with you both [Endwright and George Darling] to date. I am writing again because it seems none of your replies have advised or even addressed a number of central concerns.

I texted Caryl Churchill yesterday in a frivolous mood, asking where we had gone wrong to get four-star reviews in both the

Express and the *Telegraph*. I'm not accustomed to plaudits from the right-wing press. She responded, 'It's an old play, it's studied in schools and it's not remotely threatening any more.' This is the first point to which I would invite your response. Obviously *Top Girls* at Chichester with a current TV star in the leading role is not 'threatening', and *A Dish of Tea with Dr Johnson* is exactly what it says on the tin, 'a compassionate and entertaining literary evening'. Trudie Styler's presence as Mrs Thrale moves it from comfortable to being enticing. Of course, we have no desire or intention to 'threaten' our audiences. But some new work falls into this category. In an earlier letter I outlined our experience with *The Big Fellah* by Richard Bean, which played to the poorest houses in Bury St Edmunds that we have experienced in seventeen years of touring to that venue. The prospect of the play got extensive editorial coverage in the *Guardian*, *The Times* and the *East Anglian Times*; but the more the good citizens of Bury St Edmunds read about it, the less they wanted to see it. It was about a Republican cell in New York collecting funds for the IRA, and it sounded violent and alarming. I also mentioned that the Duke's Playhouse, Lancaster, had withdrawn from negotiations over *Bang Bang Bang* [Stella's play about human rights defenders working in the Congo began with violence and rape] as they didn't feel they could get an audience. But we don't have to be so 'threatening'. We could have done Harold Pinter's *Betrayal* with Kristin Scott Thomas, although I doubt if she would tour. Incidentally, at the moment only four of the seven actresses in *Top Girls* are prepared to consider touring when the London season is over. These are the difficulties we constantly face.

In the current year both *Top Girls* and *A Dish of Tea with Dr Johnson* are transferring to the West End. This means the 'subsidy per seat' measurement which you hold in such high esteem will be very low. This is fortuitous rather than a considered act of programming policy. But is this right? Would the Arts Council prefer us to programme less 'threatening' work? As I say, it would work wonders for the 'subsidy per seat' ratio.

The second point I have made in earlier correspondence, to which you have made no reply, is 'development'. Looking at Out of Joint's last seven productions, three have involved two-week workshops and a considerable outlay in development costs. Of the remaining four, two had public readings at a fairly minimal cost. Only two went straight into a conventional five-week rehearsal period. But *The Convict's Opera,* a substantial reworking of John Gay's *The Beggar's Opera* by Stephen Jeffreys, would certainly have benefited from the scrutiny offered by a proper workshop. This was impossible because of the distances involved in this Anglo-Australian co-production.

Of the seven projects Out of Joint are currently considering for 2012/13, only one, a non-'threatening' revival of *Our Country's Good*, a play by Timberlake Wertenbaker about the staging by early convicts in Australia of *The Recruiting Officer,* is a final script. Two need workshops before a first draft can be undertaken, and the remaining four will all require further development once the script is received. But is this a luxury we can no longer afford? As I say, we could have done *Betrayal* with Kristin Scott Thomas. Development makes Out of Joint's 'subsidy per seat' highly expensive. Should we ditch it?

Clearly you have had to take difficult decisions, and your correspondence makes great play of the 'open and fair process'. What is open about a process taken behind closed doors with no consultation, no appeal and judged by criteria we had been unaware of and which are in any case only partially relevant? About as 'fair' as the All Blacks playing a prep-school XV, and about as 'open' as Wormwood Scrubs.

We have sent you a list of 'cold spots' some time ago and eagerly await your response. I appreciate that you are unable to acknowledge that your decision to cut Out of Joint's funding is simply wrong, and that you are doing your best to work with Graham and me. But I can't stop myself asking whether you regret the publication of your absurd brochure 'Achieving Excellence for All'? Since Out of Joint's work is rated as 'great art' from your own lips, and you have assured us that the quality of work is not in question, why have you imposed a cut that will inevitably mean our excellence is confined to the few?

Should the glossy brochure not be reprinted with a new title:
'Achieving Excellence for London and One or Two Rich
Bastards in the Provinces'?

The point I was trying to make, as I pursued the 'cold spot' funding
that had appeared dagger-like before us, the handle stretched
towards our hand, was that not only had the decision to cut Out of
Joint been wrong, but that the entire system by which the decision
had been made, as it was half-explained to us—an analysis of our
work based in part on a set of mathematical equations relating to
audience figures—was based on narrow-minded, unsatisfactory criteria. Attendance is of course a priority for any artistic director—we
have our targets and monitor everything. During our respective
innings as Artistic Directors of the Royal Court, both George Devine
and I had kept notebooks in which we recorded by hand the advances
and matured figures for every performance presented—but sales
cannot be the only criteria by which touring or new writing or
'excellent' theatre (as the Arts Council deemed and continue to
deem our work) is judged. To base support primarily on attendances
is an active disincentive to creativity, risk-taking and genuine innovation, something that free-market Tories fundamentally fail to grasp,
because the bottom line remains, resolutely, their bottom line. We
on the left are not so very different to them—we want the same pio-
neering spirit they hope to instil in their bankers from our artists and
our leaders—but we believe there are criteria other than profit and
loss by which you can measure success. When David Cameron advo-
cated that the British Film Council should principally support films
that were going to make a profit, it became very clear who it was
who had pressured the Arts Council into basing their support of art
on finance. Some months later I found an interview with Tamara
Rojo in the *Guardian*. She is the Artistic Director of English National
Ballet, which had also suffered a 15% cut: 'Governments and people who take these decisions must realise that, yes, there will still be
ballet companies, but it will be increasingly rare that they are able

to take the creative risk that renews and reinvigorates an art form.' Precisely. The cuts pushed us inevitably towards conservatism. It was well understood by both ourselves and the Arts Council that Out of Joint's remit was to generate new work. By reducing this possibility were the Arts Council preparing the way to declare the whole company redundant?

With regards to cold spots, the trail itself went 'cold' in the end. The funding had been 'a dagger of the mind, a false creation'.

3rd October 2011

Dear Max,

Unfortunately, I can't give you an answer at the moment in relation to 'cold spots'. The Arts Council is currently defining where is and where isn't a cold spot (it's based on a large amount of research data). We are also refining what our expectations are in relation to engaging with 'cold spots'. We will have guidance about this later in the autumn. Until I've seen that guidance, I'm loath to make suggestions and comments. I'm sorry that that is not very helpful for you right now and your discussions with University of Hertfordshire.

After four months the Arts Council concluded that they were unable to define a 'cold spot' and that in any case Out of Joint would not qualify for extra funding from this direction. With the continued support of the University of Hertfordshire, and additional help from the National Theatre Studio, we continued to develop the project. Our interest in taking work to out-of-the-way places has never been dictated by funding, though it would have been nice to have got some for doing so.

While this campaign continued, the business of running a theatre company had to go on, of course, and as I continued to correspond with Endwright, I simultaneously embarked upon one of the busiest periods in Out of Joint's history. As soon as *Top Girls* was up and running, I turned to our production *A Dish of Tea with Dr Johnson*, a play woven out of the writings of James Boswell about the great Samuel Johnson, which we had developed the previous year in a workshop, and which had already toured the country to great acclaim. *A Dish of Tea with Dr Johnson* was to play a limited season at the Traverse Theatre in Edinburgh during the Festival, before transferring to the Arts Theatre in the West End. I had only once previously opened a show in the Arts Theatre, a revue I had directed while a student at Trinity College Dublin. The review from Milton Shulman in the *Evening Standard* has stayed with me. He wrote: 'The one good thing about this infantile undergraduate revue is that none of these young people will ever be seen in the professional theatre again.' It was therefore a particular pleasure to return to that venue almost fifty years later—and with a proven success.

Although I accept that critics and the rest of us are playing on the same team I learnt early on that they are the most unreliable and arbitrary of fellows. Someone who shows rare perception, sensitivity and insight on one occasion can prove the most terrible dunderhead when next they go out to bat.

I was to experience the quixotic and arbitrary nature of criticism some eighteen months after Milton Shulman's excoriation when I brought a Stanley Eveling play, *Dear Janet Rosenberg, Dear Mr Kooning*, to the Theatre Upstairs. The press officer at the Royal Court was Gloria Taylor. She was an ex-*Vogue* model who subsequently married into the Saudi royal family—not a career path followed by many colleagues at the Royal Court. At some point during the technical rehearsals she suggested that I should meet Harold Hobson on the press night. At the time, Harold Hobson (writing for the *Sunday Times*) and Kenneth Tynan (in the *Observer*) pretty well ruled the theatrical world. As the press night approached, I asked Gloria what my duties entailed. 'Well,' she said, 'you will have to carry him up the stairs.' I should explain that Harold Hobson was, as I am now, 'a raspberry'. He was very small, although with a perfectly normal-sized head full of brains, and he had a club foot. There was no lift in

those days, and five flights of stairs to the Theatre Upstairs. At the
appointed time I guided the enormous Daimler limousine into the
alleyway between the Royal Court and Sloane Square Tube station. I
lifted him from the front seat and carried him up the stairs. I was
young and fit, and it didn't take a feather out of me. I then returned
downstairs, went round the corner to the coffee shop in Holbein
Place, and bought two cups of tea—one for Mrs Hobson and one
for the chauffeur. At this point I must have still had some principles
of liberal socialism left!

After the performance I tenderly gathered Mr Hobson from his
seat and carried him downstairs. I recall his tweed jacket chafing my
cheek. We gossiped freely about the theatre, protocol of course pre-
venting any discussion about the play he had just seen. I put him back
in the Daimler and waved it out into Sloane Square. We hadn't discussed the play, but I knew that after the intimacy we had enjoyed
he could not but write a positive review. And so it proved. The
review began, 'Mr Eveling and Mr Stafford-Clark make the profession of drama critic the most noble known to man. All London
should pack this theatre till the walls burst.' Since the Theatre
Upstairs seated 65, his command wasn't too hard to follow, and the
theatre was duly packed. I knew that I had cheated in some obscure
way, but my only regret is that those days are gone. Now, if I'm to
attain the same intimacy with Michael Billington or Quentin Letts,
they would have to carry me. I couldn't stagger even a step or two
with Jane Edwardes or Sarah Hemming.

At the same time as *A Dish of Tea with Dr Johnson* opened, *Top Girls*
also transferred into the West End, and I went into rehearsals on
Stella's play *Bang Bang Bang*, which took me to Bolton for the final
weeks of rehearsal. It was bitterly ironic that the cut had been proposed at a moment when Out of Joint was enjoying a particularly
diverse and well-attended period of activity, and our 'subsidy per
seat' would be consequently lower than usual.

Bang Bang Bang is about the lives of human rights defenders
working for an NGO in the Congo. A further letter to Frank

Endwright after the opening in Bolton again attempted to draw out a clearer picture of what the Arts Council wanted from Out of Joint. This was, it appeared, curiously difficult to define. I returned to the point again desperate to get an answer.

10th October 2011

Dear Frank,

You will recall I endeavoured to define 'threatening new work', a phrase I had picked up from Caryl Churchill. I defined *Top Girls* and *A Dish of Tea with Dr Johnson* as being at the unthreatening and audience-friendly end of the spectrum of Out of Joint's work, whereas, whether we like it or not, the audience defined *The Big Fellah* and *Bang Bang Bang* as being 'threatening', and consequently obtaining bookings was hard and the advance was poor for those two plays. The question I wanted to put to the Arts Council, as our principal patrons, was: should we therefore programme less challenging work? Should we consider reviving *Closer*, *The Blue Room* or *Copenhagen*, or would this *not* be fulfilling our Arts Council remit? All this is making the point that some new work is more threatening than others.

This question seemed to me to be of great importance as Out of Joint sought to plan for the new financial reality. We had built a reputation based on innovation and artistic risk-taking; now we were told we weren't value for money. Should we play things safer and programme revivals rather than new plays; should we focus our efforts on luring stars into our shows? Caryl Churchill had coined the term 'unthreatening' to explain the success of *Top Girls*, an acknowledged classic. This was opposed to the 'threatening' new *The Big Fellah* by Richard Bean, which we had toured just before our cut, and Stella's own 'threatening' offering, *Bang Bang Bang*. Determining whether the Arts Council wanted us to take fewer risks or how we could spend less money continuing with our more 'threatening' agenda seemed vital for our future programming. Frank had come to rehearsals of *Bang Bang Bang*, and his subsequent letter put much faith in the efficiency of a revamped business model in raising the funds necessary for development.

15th October 2011

Dear Max,

Thank you for letting me attend rehearsals last week. They were interesting and informative as always.

We said then that it would be helpful if I wrote down the responses that I had made in our meeting to some of the issues raised in your letters. Since then, of course, you have been working on developing your business plan.

Firstly, though, I would like to thank you for continuing to engage with us, and I want to reiterate that we are committed to working with you.

Perhaps, though, it is worth going back to the art. You have argued passionately in your letters and when we have met for the importance of sufficient development/rehearsal time and for the freedom to develop work that is 'threatening'. I take that term to mean – amongst other things – provocative; shocking; bold; brave and truthful; meaningful; challenging and engaging. All these adjectives can be – and probably have been over the years – applied to your work. And it is exactly those qualities that we cherish in your work.

What you are saying very clearly is that in order to produce high-quality, 'threatening' work, you need sufficient rehearsal/development time. Following on from that, I would reiterate what I said in our meeting – that if the core purpose or mission of Out of Joint is the creation of high-quality, 'threatening' plays, then the business model and plan should be built around delivering that – and since development time is a key creative need, the model should be constructed such that it allows for that. However, I would add that in order to do this successfully, the business plan needs to be effective – at, amongst other things, marshalling resources, expending them and at generating income.

We would hope that Out of Joint will arrive at that more effective business model but we recognise that developing and implementing it will take time. As such, as we have said, it seems to make sense for you to plan for '12/13, much as you already have, based on your existing model. Graham's recent emailed '12/13 budget [enclosed in this book as Appendix 2], based as it is on the one production, would seem predicated on that. This seems sensible as long as it coincides with progress on the development of a new business plan.

The desire from the Arts Council seemed to be for more of the same from us, but with less of the same from them. Having been unable to define 'cold spots', it now also seemed that the word 'threatening' was proving difficult too, so I sought to resolve this, not wishing them to pigeonhole Out of Joint purely as an antagonistic organisation, a theatrical IRA.

22nd October 2011

Dear Frank,

Thanks for resending your email of 15th October. I see it answers some but not all of the points I was striving to make. 'Threatening' was Caryl Churchill's phrase not mine, and she used it to make the point that *Top Girls* was threatening in 1982 but was no longer so in 2011. I borrowed her terminology to make the point that some work in the spectrum of plays we produce is deemed 'threatening' by the audience. I didn't intend it to be a qualitative judgement: 'threatening' plays can be terrible, and of course 'non-threatening' plays can be terrific. One conclusion even a peremptory study of Out of Joint's history yields is that revivals (*Three Sisters*, *She Stoops to Conquer*, *Macbeth*) do well at the box office, as do new plays set in the past (i.e. costume dramas). So *Our Country's Good*, *Our Lady of Sligo*, *Andersen's English*, *The Libertine* and

A Dish of Tea with Dr Johnson have all done well for us at the box office in London and regionally. Whereas on the other hand, *Talking to Terrorists*, a verbatim play by Robin Soans, *The Big Fellah* and, currently, *Bang Bang Bang* have all performed poorly in the regions until they have had the imprimatur of London reviews and approval. It remains, I believe, a valuable strand of our work, but this 'threatening' work has been shown to wreak havoc with our 'subsidy per seat' ratio. You came to some rehearsals of *Bang Bang Bang*, which is touring regionally before it plays a season in London at the Royal Court Theatre Upstairs. The advances regionally and in London are in marked contrast. The season Upstairs has been sold out for the last month, while the advances in Oxford, Southampton and Leicester have been conspicuously poor. The performances so far have been very well received regionally. I think the play and the production are excellent and exemplify the very best of Out of Joint's work. This is, of course, a totally subjective judgement which you are at liberty to disregard, but it is backed by the opinions of David Thacker, the Octagon's Artistic Director, Patrick Sandford, Artistic Director of the Nuffield Theatre, Southampton, and Iain Gillie at the Leicester Curve. It is also augmented by the four post-show discussions I have attended in those theatres we have toured to. These have without doubt been the most interesting and involved I have ever known, and audiences have engaged with the provocative questions thrown up by the play as well as commenting on the power and excellence of the play itself. It remains nonetheless in the 'threatening' area of work that we produce, and regional attendance will reflect this. So, the question I reiterate is, should we steer away from programming this sort of work? Clearly it has damaged our relationship with the Arts Council, since you justify the brutal cut we have sustained by pointing to the poor attendance or 'subsidy per seat' ratio, as you believe you can get 'better value' new work elsewhere. Your words.

Nor is this a new dilemma for the Arts Council. It's one your organisation has addressed since its inception. David Kynaston's *Austerity Britain* has a fascinating chapter on the cultural ambitions of the Arts Council when it was founded and the subsequent disappointment at attendance nationwide. The Arts Council and its big brothers, the NHS and the New Towns, were all children of the extraordinary post-war Attlee government. The desire to turn the urban proletariat into a culture-conscious class of opera lovers and theatregoers was, unsurprisingly, never fulfilled, but after flirting with amateur theatre in its initial years, the Arts Council put its weight behind the repertory movement and was quick to respond to a change of direction with the fertility and energy of fringe companies, including Joint Stock, in the sixties and seventies. I recall that Joint Stock had only been in existence for one year before it received the guarantee of regular funding.

It took a conscious effort at first to adopt a civil tone in my letters to Frank Endwright. Dr Johnson famously described a patron as 'one who looks with unconcern at a man struggling for life in the water, and when he reaches ground at last, encumbers him about with help,' but this acutely punishing, devastating and abrupt rejection from our principal patron felt very much like being thrown back into the water. It had become clear that they wanted us to continue to programme 'threatening' work, but to find the money for it ourselves from the miracle-making new business model we were to devise. It was difficult not to feel angry and hurt by that 'unconcern'. Perhaps the Arts Council's cut seemed a form of paternal rejection. I reacted to it particularly sharply because it was a new experience for me.

*

I had always enjoyed wholehearted parental support. My father Max had directed a play while he was reading agriculture at Reading University before the war, and my young cousin, Sebastian, who lives in Australia, is currently studying at NIDA, so maybe there's a soupçon of theatrical inclination in the family. My father David was enormously encouraging. He and my mother came to every production during my time at the Royal Court as he had once come to every rugby match I played. He once said to me, 'Max, I don't know exactly what you do as a director, but I do know you do it extremely well.'

As you may have spotted, I had two fathers, which may be why I find the father-son relationship so interesting. Some weekend in the summer of 1937 my father David drove down to Lodge Farm near Aston Clinton in Buckinghamshire and played tennis against a friend from medical school, Ian Stewart. Ian's younger brother, my father Max, was umpire and ballboy, having left Berkhamsted School that summer. The striking Victorian farmhouse is built high in the Chiltern Hills up one side of the valley. As you drive down the Icknield Way from Wendover to Tring it stands above the road on a terrace carved into the side of the hill. It's a spectacular setting. The hill was terraced before the Romans and the Romans themselves grew grapes in the shallow chalk soil on the sunny, south-facing slopes. The tennis court was special too. It had been rolled and laid by Ian, and it stood in the orchard field at the bottom of the valley. The small orchard had apples, pears and plums, and the tennis court stood some way off near the wood that continued up the valley. A small chalk quarry had chiselled away one side of the hill. This was the site of the tennis court, and the sharp incline acted as a wall to prevent over-hit balls from going too far out of court. A ballboy was essential as there were no side nets, just a five-bar Victorian iron fence moved from elsewhere on the farm to keep the cows from the close-cut grass. My grandfather had a fine dairy herd, and the farm still did a milk round until 1949. I remember watching the cream rise in the great zinc pails in the dairy. I don't know who won the game, but I'm sure it was fiercely competitive. My uncle was the better athlete—he had played fly half for Guy's Hospital—but my father David was the better tennis player and was very keen. Max was three years younger than David so although they were friendly, at twenty-one and eighteen, the age gap was too great for a close friendship. But they met on at least that one occasion. And they liked each other.

My father Max met my mother on a train. He was with the Royal Suffolks and was returning to the regimental HQ in Bury St

Edmunds, while my mother was also making for Bury where she was a staff nurse at the Suffolk General. She and a girlfriend had been to the theatre in London. The train was slow and it was, of course, blacked out, so she and Max can't have had much opportunity to look at each other on the long journey from Liverpool Street. But Max had a bad cold, and, as always, my mother was armed with tissues. This I believe was the foundation of their relationship. My mother and her friend had a taxi waiting to take them to the Nurses' Home in Bury St Edmunds, and they gave Max a lift. The next day he turned up at the hospital with flowers. He didn't know my mother's full name so he could only identify her to the hospital secretary as 'the staff nurse with stunning red hair named Dorothy'. The matron came herself to find my mother on the ward. She reported that there was a young man to see her. My mother said she knew of no young men in Bury. 'Oh, but you do, nurse,' riposted the matron. 'Either that or you have inherited a flower shop.'

My mother came from Worksop in Nottinghamshire where her father was a tailor. Moments of prosperity came for him only when there was a pit disaster and men had to order suits for the funerals. It's hard to think of Max and Dorothy meeting outside the particular circumstances and social confusion caused by the war. Certainly their courtship was swift and they married without letting either of their respective families know. I don't think it was particularly clandestine, but it was war and behavioural norms were suspended. Max proposed to her in Lavenham sitting in the market square in his blue 1932 Austin 7. Lavenham is beautiful. The secluded market square is up a slight incline above the high street. There's a half-timbered medieval guildhall and a fine old pub where they later stayed for the one night of their honeymoon. Both were in a state of pleasured shock at falling in love for the first time. Max wrote to a friend:

I am very pleased that I married her, though Lodge Farm has scarcely recovered from the shock of being presented with the 'fait accompli'. I have felt a little guilty towards

> my parents in this matter, but the war has made everything
> so difficult that I think perhaps our selfishness was
> justifiable.

Justifiable... and short. Between the marriage and Max's death there were half a dozen occasions when he had leave and they could be together. My mother didn't meet her parents-in-law until the funeral. When she gave birth to me three and a half months later, she had at her side the same friend who had been present when she met Max on the train. It had been less than a year earlier. They had met in April. Max was in France through May and was evacuated from France on June 4th, and they were married two weeks later on June 17th. He was killed on November 29th and I was born on 17th March 1941. It wasn't until I visited his grave with my mother years later that I fully absorbed this information from the inscribed stone and realised how headlong their romance had been. What a bold decision they had taken. In 1940 it was a vote for life. Perhaps Max had been shocked by his experiences in France. Dunkirk is remembered somehow as a victory, at least for British courage and determination. But at the time it was a humiliating defeat. It must even have seemed the end. One survivor remembers:

> We were lost for words. I don't know how else to put it.
> We were just so devastated and humiliated. I could not
> believe how well equipped the Germans were. They were
> prepared for war and we weren't.

Max won an MC at Dunkirk. It was for crucially delaying the German advance and allowing his men to escape that chaos with their lives and weapons intact. Army form W3121 for the award of his Military Cross says:

2/Lt Stewart was commanding a platoon of the forward
company. He was at work with the majority of his platoon
on the preparation for final closing of the main roadblock,
when the enemy suddenly appeared and opened fire. He
immediately took his men back to their positions. He then
returned with his orderly to the roadblock and completed
the closing and mining of it under mortar and machine
gunfire. A little later an enemy tank was put out of action
by the mines he had placed at the roadblock.

Back in Bury St Edmunds he got married immediately. After the
marriage he wrote to a friend:

Don't you yourself feel that this year has done much to
arrest reflection and thought? Of course it has. One lives
now from day to day – soon it will be from hour to hour
with no thought of the future because that future is so
dully obscure.

Of course I never knew my father Max. But he has always been a
presence: on my mother's dressing table and on the piano at Lodge
Farm is the same studio portrait of him in army uniform with the
captain's pips on his shoulder and his cap slightly slanted, sending a
shadow across his face. Bits of him have kept surfacing all through
my life. One holiday at Lodge Farm I found his name carved deep in
a chestnut tree. I must have been about eight. When I was seventeen
I inherited the 1932 Austin 7, GO 3749, that had once been his and
in which he proposed to my mother. And in 1998 I was given this
letter. It was addressed to me and had been written by Max's old
headmaster at Berkhamsted School. He must have written it when I
was about three. He gave it to Wren, Max's younger brother, who
passed it on to me fifty-five years later:

I am writing this in order that you may know something of
what your father was in the eyes of those who knew him
best when he was a boy at Berkhamsted. I hope when you
have read this you will realise you have indeed reason to be
proud of being his son. He came to this school in 1926
when he was only eight years old, and when he left in 1937
he held the position of Head Prefect. As Headmaster I
want to say that I have never known a senior boy whom I
trusted, nor one who served his house and his school,
more loyally. He was outstandingly good as an athlete and
was captain of rugby football, of swimming and of gym.
He was the senior Under-Officer in the OTC. At the same
time he was possessed of considerable literary ability and
won the Fry Memorial Essay prize, while he also became
Editor of the *Berkhamstedian*. I don't believe there was
anyone in the school, Master or boy or school servant,
who did not admire and respect him. His absolute sincerity
and transparent honesty and a willingness at times to give
anyone a helping hand were the qualities that made him
what he was.

A Headmaster owes many things to his boys but never a
greater debt than I owed to your father. I am proud to
know that we were friends. You indeed have the best
inheritance of all—a grand character.

C.M. Cox
Headmaster

My father David had also been involved in the retreat from France,
and on June 17th, the day Dorothy and Max got married, he was
supervising the sabotage of ambulances, tankers, staff cars and a can-
teen truck at the small port of La Pallice, just south of La Rochelle.
They were driven off the quay into the water and that night he
wrote, 'Sailed under Stuka attack out of La Pallice 23:30.' When

David qualified as a doctor in 1940 he had immediately joined the RAF and had gone to France with 73 Squadron of Fighter Command as a medical officer. After Dunkirk the Germans began to overrun the rest of France and the Hurricane squadron retreated through Le Mans, Saumur and Nantes to La Pallice, covering the fleeing army. The RAF were blamed for not providing sufficient air cover at Dunkirk. 'I feel very deeply about this BEF [British Expeditionary Force] security,' wrote David in his journal. 'The young pilots have done sheer wonders against incredible odds… but they were high up and often trying to intercept bombers fifty miles away and en route for Dunkirk—so BEF on beachhead might well not see them.' The Hurricanes flew back to Church Fenton in Yorkshire, leaving the ground personnel to get out as best they could. In La Pallice the RAF commandeered two colliers which had brought coal for the French railways over from Monmouthshire. The journey back to Newport took five days: on the second day one of the colliers was torpedoed by a U-boat which was in turn sunk by a Sunderland. The remaining collier, now crammed with men who had to sleep on the piles of coal, had to stand to outside Newport for two days while the Docks were swept for magnetic mines. Filthy and demoralised, the RAF men were booed by the dockers in Newport as they disembarked.

David transferred to Bomber Command and, while on a course at RAF Halton, called in at Lodge Farm two miles away. He knew Max had been killed and that his elder brother Ian was missing, presumed captured, after the fall of Crete. But David had heard through the Red Cross that Ian was on a prisoner-of-war list, and when he called in at the farmhouse, it was to give my grandparents this good news. There he met my mother for the first time. She was a widow of five months. He wrote in his journal:

Decided to call in at Lodge Farm on my way through Tring. I had tea with Mr and Mrs Stewart. Wren and Rhona were there… also was a girl called Dorothy—Max's widow—with a six-week-old baby. She impressed me tremendously.

So lovely, so poised, so charming, so sweet with her baby,
and beautiful to see. I love her. Fundamental admission.

He wrote me a poem too. Like Max, David had literary ambitions
and had won the Gate Prize for Poetry while he was still at school.
This poem was never published, but I found it written in rough in his
diary for 29th April 1941, the day of my christening.

You are not old yet Max
Six weeks is no great age, even in war
When I was six weeks old
Europe was shuddering to the guns
As they smashed the men fighting for Verdun

People were tense and anxious then—as now
But 'Ils ne passeront pas…' men said:
And that time they were right.
Yet now they have passed and they've taken France—
I saw them do it.

As I grew older, I heard about The War,
And I used to play at it in a garden
With my brother John…
Oh how we loved that game
Eleven and seven we were.

But it was strange and sad, for those who knew
        better
To see us tumbling dead or wounded in the long
        grass.
Looking at us, their hearts sick with a sudden dread
They said 'Pray God they'll never grow to know it
        better…'
Looking at you, I long to add my promise to that
        prayer.

Later he had two volumes of poetry published. This one is included in an anthology of Second World War poetry, and describes how David spent the war. It's called 'Casualty':

'Easy boys, leave it to the Doc...
Afraid he's pretty bad, doc; we've not heard
A word from him since just before we bombed...'
Hands under his arms and knees
Lift him down gently; unplug his intercom
And disconnect his oxygen.
Now guide his shoulders and dislodge his feet
From the wrecked turret;
So lay him down and look at him.

'Much you can do?
          'No I'm afraid he's dead,
Has been for hours—' 'Oh. Well I'm sorry—'
                                    'Yes,
Probably never knew what hit him.'
But in the torchlight you can see
His face is frozen;
Cannon shells pumped into his side
From neck to knee. Skin white like frozen lard,
Eyes glazed, with frosted lashes,
Flying suit crusted with red chalk
That was his blood...
          Such is the cold
In a smashed turret open to the wind
Torn at that height and speed through icy darkness.
Yesterday
I heard someone complain
'Last night the bombers in procession
Kept me awake.'

As senior medical officer on a Heavy Bomber station he had to deal not only with the shrapnel wounds, broken limbs and terrible burns sustained during operational sorties, but also with the collapse in morale occasioned by the hideous dangers to which the flying men were exposed. He wrote:

> The chances of any particular individual surviving his thirty trips alive, unwounded and without having been forced down over enemy territory were generally accepted by the aircrew themselves as being just about one in five.

He flew with them as often as he could, and they found he had both a compassionate and sympathetic ear and an imaginative and intuitive grasp of the damage to the mind that this unbearable stress could cause.

'What were these incidents like?' he wrote.

> They were like nothing else in the world. The aircrew flew in darkness relieved only by the dim orange glow of a lamp over the navigator's table and the faintly green luminosity of the pilot's instruments, three or four miles high through bitter cold over hundreds of miles of sea and hostile land, with the thunderous roaring of the engine shutting out all other sounds except when the crackling metallic voice of one member of the crew echoed in the other's earphones. For each man there was a constant awareness of danger; danger from the enemy; the sudden blinding convergence of searchlights accompanied by heavy, accurate and torrential flak; from packs of night fighters seeking unceasingly to find and penetrate the bomber stream; of danger from collision, from ice in the cloud, from becoming lost or isolated, from a chance hit in a petrol tank leading to loss of fuel and a forced

descent into the sea. There was no single moment of security from take-off to touch-down, but often the sight of
another aircraft hit by flak and exploding in the air, of plum-
meting down blazing to strike the ground an incandescent
wreck. These were the familiar aspects of the flying man's
experience. To these he had to adapt himself so that he could
eat, sleep, read, work and play, not unaffected by them—
that would be impossible—but undefeated by them.

That's an extract from his MD thesis written after the war, called
'Morale and Flying Experience'. Airmen whose morale had been
shattered and who could no longer fly were deemed to have 'L.M.F'.
The letters stood for 'Low Moral Fibre', and an earlier version of
David's paper induced the Air Ministry to drop the term and to treat
sufferers with more understanding and less opprobrium.

His stories of the war fascinated me. It must have been both
extraordinary and horrible to live so intensely with death as a constant presence. As Robert E. Lee wrote, 'It is well that war is so
terrible, otherwise we should grow too fond of it.' Both my fathers
had their share of the terrible in France. David writes of freeing a
dead pilot from the burnt wreck of a Hurricane: 'I extricated the
charred corpse with trailing entrails and brittle limbs.' Max and his
frightened platoon were jeered by French soldiers who had already
given up as both groups retreated towards Cherbourg. The French
were drinking wine on a bridge over a small river, and Max seized
the bottles and threw them in the water.

His RAF experiences led David towards psychiatry when his
medical career resumed after the war. He told me that in the 1950s,
psychiatry had seemed the Africa of medicine. He meant it was the
dark continent where a young man could make his reputation as an
explorer of the unknown. He said he had become a doctor so he
could be the person who made his way through the crowd in the
event of an accident. He had a strong element of the showman about
him. I remember seeing him on a ward round looking like a medieval

duke surrounded by a court of nurses and junior doctors, elegant in
a snappy striped suit with a brocaded waistcoat. He was a brilliant
speaker, and his lectures to the medical school at Guy's were vivid,
clear and hugely entertaining. The students thundered their boots on
the floor of the lecture hall in approbation, but at the same time he
was entirely focused on persuading young doctors to remove the
stigma and alarm that had long been associated with mental illness
and its treatment. My own later steps towards the theatre were ten-
tative enough, but they met with no opposition from him. It was a
career he admired and would have liked in some form for himself.

But if my mother's engagement to Max had been spectacularly
short, her courtship with David was protracted. She expressed no
desire to marry again but David was tenacious and determined. Having been turned down on three occasions he arrived on the fourth
without his beautiful, pre-war, two-seater Singer. He explained that
he had sold it and exchanged it for a family car. My mother pointed
out that he did not have a family. 'I'm in the process of acquiring one,'
said David. It's clear that he saw his commitment to this young
widow and her child as a personal declaration of permanence in a
world that had revealed itself as slippery and dangerous. His own
beloved younger brother, John, had been killed at the end of February 1941. During training with the RNAS the wing fell off his
Liberator. David kept his watch in a drawer of his desk, a smashed
and mangled icon. His entry in his diary that day reads simply, 'My
brother Jonathan, best loved man in life, was killed today flying.'
When my parents finally did get married in December 1942, my
name was changed in the High Court. With one father's name leading from the front and with another's shepherding me from behind,
I acquired the lengthy label I have always carried through life:
Maxwell Robert Guthrie Stewart Stafford-Clark. But this decision,
which came from David's desire to make me a complete part of any
future family he and my mother might have, offended the Stewarts
mightily. With one son killed and another in a prisoner-of-war camp
I represented the future. They were angry and distraught.

The rift between the families wasn't healed until the war was over. In fact, my earliest memory is of driving from where we lived in Bognor Regis to Lodge Farm. I was four, and, before motorways, it was a prodigious cross-country trek for the Morris, EYY 814. Then, as now, junior doctors were overworked and underpaid. We lived in a pleasant enough semi-detached suburban house, but Lodge Farm, although not palatial, was certainly the grandest house that I had ever seen. With its own driveway that wound up the hill from the farmyard, it was in a class of its own. The house had, and still has, a small conservatory that encloses the front door. As the car came to a halt after our epic journey the doors burst open and seven or eight farm dogs came bustling down the drive in friendly greeting, wagging their tails and barking. Behind them came a small, grey-haired woman of some elegance who pelted down the drive and swept me up in her arms. She was weeping. Great tears were cascading down her cheeks, the dogs were barking, everyone was talking and I too burst into sympathetic and overwhelmed tears. This was the reconciliation. And this was my grandmother, Kitty.

When I was six, David explained to me why I had an extra set of grandparents. I don't think this was a situation I had examined fully, although it seemed of great convenience on occasions like Christmas or birthdays. It was an important moment to him. We were driving down to North Devon now in the Standard Vanguard, KPX 399, and had stopped for a break outside Honiton. We walked across a meadow and sat on a fence overlooking a railway cutting. David said he had something important to tell me. He said that I had another daddy, Max, who I was named after, that he had been terribly brave and that he had been killed in the war, but how important I was to him, David, and how he would always love me just as much as Scylla, my sister, and as much indeed as any other brothers or sisters who might be in the pipeline, so to speak. I think my mother was pregnant with my brother Jonathan at the time, and that's why she wasn't there. However, I was fully engaged with developing a deep and abiding love for steam engines and don't remember the occasion at all. I can only write about it because it was such a vivid memory for David who told me of it on many occasions. He remembered everything: my hand in his crossing the meadow, the grass, the fence, the afternoon sun, the impressive steam engines and my response. Apparently I said I didn't mind a bit but I was sure from the information he had given me that Max would have been a nice daddy too, perhaps even as nice as he, David, was, which was very nice indeed.

I chose to forget all this and when people asked in later years if David was in fact my stepfather or if Jonathan and Nigel were my stepbrothers I denied it firmly. I wanted to be a fully paid-up member of this family and wouldn't contemplate any half-measures.

I was ambushed some years later when I was fourteen or fifteen. I was at boarding school in Felsted in Essex. I found public school a chronic condition of low-level misery, and am at one with Evelyn Waugh when he writes, 'Anyone who has been to an English public school will always feel comparatively at home in a prison.' I survived because I was good at games, but this particular afternoon it was CCF, which wasn't so enjoyable. We were taking Cert A Part 2, some form of cadet exam whose purpose now eludes me. We had done map-reading, drill, assembly of a light machine gun and doubtless other arduous tasks and there remained only an initiative test. We were made to wait in the indoor swimming pool and were summoned out one by one to be questioned by an officer from the Travelling Wing, who had come down to examine us. This particular afternoon the officers were from the Royal Suffolk Regiment. It was a clear, cold February afternoon, and I was one of the last to be summoned. The winter light was fading when my turn arrived. The officer stood under a tree in his greatcoat with a clipboard. He checked off my name and looked up. The fading light slanted across his face. Suddenly I knew exactly who he was. It was Max. He had the same coat, the same cap badge, the same pips on his shoulder. I was stunned. He asked me a question. I heard it clearly but was quite incapable of any response. He repeated the question: 'You're on guard duty. Your mate has gone for a pee. Somebody comes into the guardroom in civvies. You don't recognise them. They're probably from another regiment. They don't remember the password. They're drunk and abusive. What do you do?' As I looked at him, great choking sobs welled up in my throat. Puzzled, he repeated the question again. 'Well, would you shoot him?' he asked pleasantly enough. Sobs which I tried to disguise as laughter burst from me. The young captain was concerned at my inexplicable behaviour, but the kinder he became the worse it got. By now I was blubbing quite openly. 'Well, you'd ring for help, wouldn't you?' he finally prompted. 'Yes,' I shouted in a flash flood of snot and tears. He gave me a pass and let me go. God knows what he made of it all. I ran back across the damp playing fields and stuffed the incident back in my subconscious where it was to stay for many years.

'You can no more win a war than you can win an earthquake,' said Jeanette Rankin, the American pacifist. As he got older the war became more and more vivid in David's memory, and it began to seem like a war that he had lost. It was a monument that grew bigger in his life as he gave up medicine and the other landmarks receded. He was sometimes angry at the waste of life and often bitter at the futility of it. The last time I saw David I had come down to Brighton to take my mother shopping. 'How are you today?' I asked. He was reading in his study as I looked in on him with the car keys in my hand. He didn't drive the Rover 216, K127 KSR, any more. He was reading. 'Oh, I'm feeling a bit sad today, Maxie,' he said. 'I've been thinking of those fine fellows who were killed in the war. Your father, of course, and John, my brother.' When I came back from the shopping he was asleep on the sofa. The book he had been reading so studiously lay open on his desk. It was a road map of France, but on it he had carefully traced the route he had taken in 1940. Le Mans, Saumur, Nantes, La Rochelle, La Pallice. The dates and stopping places were carefully inked in.

*

As our busy 2011 season drew to a close, with successful West End runs for *Top Girls* and *A Dish of Tea with Dr Johnson* and a sell-out run in the Theatre Upstairs of *Bang Bang Bang* buoying the company, I tried (and failed) to draw together a reasonably objective annual summary of Out of Joint's work, which was our customary practice. At the same time I finally got a more informative letter from Endwright, which made some mild criticisms of *Bang Bang Bang*. I was too much in love with *Bang Bang Bang* to digest his insipid observations very easily.

28th October 2011

Dear Frank,

I must confess that I have heretofore found it hard to embrace a mutual and frank relationship with a Relationship Manager who has actively supported, nay perhaps even instigated, such a traumatic and damaging blow to the company's productivity and its morale. As I think I may have said in one of our meetings, it made me think seriously for a day or two of throwing in the towel and ending the company's existence. But Graham urges me to think afresh and move on, and I am determined to embrace his advice and embrace The Relationship and the Relationship Manager. So you may find yourself overwhelmed with friendly (and unthreatening) information.

Well, to start with, it has been a year of extraordinary and exhausting activity for the company which has stretched our resources and capabilities to the utmost. I think it has also shown to great advantage the reach and range of the company's work. April began with the Irish leg of Richard Bean's play *The Big Fellah*. It was good to take the play to Ireland and salutary to play under a commercial management with commercial expectations. In Dublin we played to an average of 265 paying punters per night and the tour concluded with successful weeks in Liverpool (217) and Newcastle (227). My own conviction is that 200 paying punters per night is a desirable and attainable target for Out of Joint.

The Big Fellah was followed by casting for *Bang Bang Bang* before *Top Girls* began rehearsals in Chichester on 6th June. This received excellent notices both on its Chichester opening (272 people per night) and on its August transfer to the Trafalgar Studios (220 people per night). The notices were unanimously approving, but irritating also: would that that level of attention and seriousness were applied to new work.

A Dish of Tea with Dr Johnson did not fare so well. The play rehearsed for its final week in Tuscany where Trudie Styler was holidaying with her children. [I had first met Trudie Styler when she was a young actress in Jonathan Gems' play *Naked Robots* at the ICA. Subsequently she had worked several times at the Royal Court. Our lives had gone in very different directions, but in 2007 she got in touch again to ask if I could advise her daughter, Mickey, who had started a career as an actor. Trudie was married to Sting, and had become an internationally known and iconic personality herself. We became friends once more. She took the role of Mrs Thrale in *Dr Johnson*, to which she most appropriately brought elegance and grace.] But one actor became severely ill in Italy and was admitted to a local hospital. *Dr Johnson* opened the next week in Edinburgh to a sold-out run at the Traverse but by this time the poor actor was in the Victoria Infirmary, Glasgow. The various expedients tried (actors reading from scripts) got us through the week but the quality of the evening was seriously affected. At the same time I was in Bolton opening *Bang Bang Bang* and, although I visited Edinburgh for a weekend, was only able to monitor the various emergency decisions from a distance. Finally, Luke Griffin was summoned from Dublin to take over the role. Inevitably it was some time before he was off the book and it was not until the final week of the four-week run at the Arts Theatre (145 people per night) that the play re-attained its quality.

Bang Bang Bang opened at the Octagon Theatre in Bolton on 5th September, where it ran for two weeks. The support we received from the Bolton technical staff was exemplary, and the run (140 people per night) was both well attended and enthusiastically reviewed. Subsequent tour weeks in Oxford (69 people per night), Southampton (109 people per night), and Leicester (73 people per night) also received excellent reviews and an enthusiastic response, but the size of the audiences was disappointing. In Southampton, for example, audiences had been 196 for *Mixed Up North* in 2009 and 159 for *Dreams of Violence* in the same year. Iain Gillie at the Leicester Curve, Patrick Sandford at the Nuffield Southampton and Lucy Maycock at the North Wall Arts Centre in Oxford were incredibly enthusiastic, not just about *Bang Bang Bang* in particular, but about the values and variety Out of Joint brought to their programming. The run at the Royal Court was a different experience. To start with, the run had been booked solid for the month before we opened and returns were hard to come by – 86 paying punters per night represented an attendance of 95.6%. The small space and the packed audiences gave a particular intensity to the experience. However, we once again suffered from illness, as Dan Fredenburgh lost his voice and was unable to perform for a week. Again he was replaced by an actor reading the script. This is never terribly satisfactory. Ironically, in the one Out of Joint production where understudies were available, *Top Girls*, they were never used.

The reviews initially failed to reach my own expectations of the evening, but we ended with four stars from *The Times,* the *Sunday Times, Time Out* and the *Sunday Express*. You write, 'I felt there was a world you wanted to explore more – the warlord, the mother and baby, the Congolese people.' You're not alone in this opinion; Michael Billington's review made many of the same points. However, I have to say I find these reservations insipid, irrelevant and misconceived. In yesterday's *Guardian*, Stephen Sondheim wrote: 'A good critic is someone who recognises and acknowledges the artist's intentions and the work's aspirations, and judges the work by them, not by what his own objectives would have been.' Carping about *Bang Bang Bang* not being about the Congo is like criticising the Great Western Railway for not going to Scotland! *Bang*

Bang Bang is a Royal Court work play which reveals the dangers and the excitement of the human rights defender as surely as David Storey's *The Changing Room* takes us into the world of rugby league. [In the fifties and sixties, the Royal Court had pioneered several plays which placed the action in the workplace and sought to show protagonists in a working environment.] You conclude, 'Nevertheless, a good production: well done!' This is quite kind, and I realise selective quoting of reviews proves little, but you will excuse me if I prefer the *Salisbury Journal*'s 'A remarkable piece of theatre; the cast is superb, the staging seamless and the direction is inspired.' As for the people on the ground, yesterday Stella Feehily received this email from a young woman who has worked in Congo for ten years:

Dear Ms Feehily,

As an Irishwoman who has worked for ten years in NGOs in eastern DRC, who bought black babies when I was a young wan with the nuns, whose nana always made my vegetarian friends eat ham sandwiches, and who has just brought her young, photographer niece to stay with her in Goma and visit mines in Masisi, I watched *Bang Bang Bang* in Salisbury on Saturday night with my heart in my mouth, and tears in my eyes.

I don't know how you did it. I swear you reached into my life and pulled it out of me, and put it on stage.

What an utterly extraordinary play. Your insights, humour, grit and messages are so true, so real, that I was grounded and transported in equal measure. The cast was fantastic, but the play was the star.

Stunning. Thank you.

Karen Hayes, MBA
Director of Artisanal Mining, Africa Region
Pact

Following the London run, reviews have again been ecstatic in Exeter (137 people per night) and in Salisbury (177 people per night to date). The response to the London reviews has made for much more satisfactory figures, although both fall some way short of our proclaimed target of 200 people per night and both represent a tangible reduction on figures we would have expected at the same venues two or three years ago.

On 29th October we borrowed the bar at the Royal Court to launch our Friends scheme. It was an excellent occasion. As to date, 21 people have joined the scheme and paid a total of £3,266. We have also intensified and increased our educational outreach and workshop programme. In the period between 1st November and the end of this financial year we will have conducted 24 workshops in three different countries, on plays ranging from *The Tempest* to *Our Country's Good* to *Rita, Sue and Bob Too* by Andrea Dunbar, and attendees range from Oxford undergraduates to Danish playwrights to professional German actors. I estimate this will raise £4,400 for Out of Joint. Both the Friends scheme and the expanded educational programme are labour intensive; many work hours will have gone into them and while the financial results are satisfactory it would be fanciful to imagine that they will in any substantial way be able to balance the lost £130,000. [One of the Arts Council's strictures was that we should diversify and increase our different income streams.]

I conclude with the rather depressing thought that once the tour of *Top Girls* opens in Warwick in the middle of January I will not be going into rehearsal again until the beginning of August. However, I will be undertaking a great deal of development work in the first half of 2012/13. The long-term objective will be to have two plays ready to go into rehearsal in 2013/14.

In fact, by Christmas 2012 we had three plays that had been at different stages of development and that were now ready to go into production. However, all three were dependent on co-production agreements; with the National Theatre, the RSC and the National

Theatre of Wales respectively. So *Pitcairn*, *Crouch, Touch, Hold, Engage* and *This May Hurt A Bit* would all have to wait. The three seemed to characterise Out of Joint's particular house style and singular approach. One was an illumination of a particular and fascinating historical moment, that is the chaos and dystopia that followed Fletcher Christian's attempt to establish a utopia on Pitcairn; the second was an account of the pressures of a particular and enclosed Welsh community and one remarkable man's response to that; and *This May Hurt A Bit* was a contribution to one of the most animated and concerted debates of our time: the future of the NHS. All very pertinent, and very Out of Joint. I continued to inform Frank Endwright of Out of Joint's activity for the rest of the year.

19th December 2011

Dear Frank,

This is the first day off I've had for two weeks and the first thing I do is sit down and write to you! That's how important I believe an ongoing relationship between Arts Council England and Out of Joint is. In my last postcard I said you or your colleagues would be made very welcome at the rehearsals of *Top Girls*. [I was engaged in re-rehearsing *Top Girls* for its Out of Joint regional tour.] You haven't replied but I repeat the invitation: we rehearse at Out of Joint's rehearsal rooms from 10 till 6 p.m. (10 till 1 on Saturdays) and our Christmas break is from Saturday 24th December to Monday 2nd January. We resume on 3rd January and we go up to Warwick on Monday 16th January. You don't have to let me know when you are coming; just turn up. I am also coaching a young woman from Camden School for Girls on her audition pieces for drama school in the evenings. Out of Joint receive no payment for this, but it is an example of the service we provide to the community.

The first week's rehearsal has gone well, and I've been lucky with a very talented cast. Advance bookings appear to be building quite nicely: as we suspected, clearly it's going to be a different story to *The Big Fellah* or *Bang Bang Bang*. As you may imagine it will be a sombre and contemplative Christmas for all of us who work at Out of Joint: those who haven't taken a voluntary salary cut for 2012/13 will be at a standstill. We have been accustomed in the past to having a staff Christmas lunch in a neighbourhood restaurant: not this year. More seriously, our practice over the last several years has been to top up the royalties of writers whose plays we produce to a figure nearing £20,000. (This includes all payments for commissioning and rehearsal attendance.) This has enabled us to compete with the Royal Court, the National and even with television companies and was, for example, directly responsible for Out of Joint obtaining the rights to *The Big Fellah*. I have already written to you about commissions, and it alarms me that we will no longer be able to maintain our standard of payments to writers. I was sharply reminded of this at the weekend when the BBC and More4 broadcast 4 hours of Andrea Dunbar's work: screening a double dose of *The Arbor* and *Rita, Sue and Bob Too*. When I commissioned Andrea she was a sixteen-year-old single mother living in horrendous conditions on a bleak council estate. Nearly thirty years on, the work has endured and become a vital social document about the underclass under Thatcher. Part of Out of Joint's original artistic manifesto was that we would undertake work that 'explored the problems and possibilities of our time'. Together with the National and the Royal Court I believe we remain one of the few companies who have the ability to place new work in the national repertoire.

The workshop on *Witches* (to be written by Rebecca Lenkiewicz) has now been fixed for the weeks of 6th and 13th February. Funding for this has been obtained both from the University of Hertfordshire and the National Theatre Studio. Over Christmas my mind will turn to other development projects. For a year I have been talking to Frank McGuinness about an adaptation or version of George Farquhar's first play *Love and a Bottle* (1698). We had agreed that Frank would write a version that directly incorporated both biographical elements of Farquhar's life, and also characters from Farquhar's second play, *The Twin Rivals*. In fact, Frank exceeded his brief by some distance and wrote a completely new play, *A Thirsty Man is Georgie,* that contained few elements of Farquhar's original play. After some discussion we agreed to go our separate ways: Frank would retain the rights to *A Thirsty Man is Georgie,* and I would seek a new writer for the adaptation. I have now approached Patrick Marber, who will read the original over Christmas. He has been writing film scripts for some years and says he has been completely blocked as a playwright. Nevertheless, I am hopeful that this may be a project that will reclaim him for the stage. I have also re-read a play of Judy Upton's, *Gaby Goes Global*, that I first came across some years ago. It contains a terrific leading role for a middle-aged actress to play a clerk at an employment office who becomes an enormously successful art-gallery entrepreneur. If we can find a star also interested (Miranda Hart, Dawn French, Miriam Margolyes, Celia Imrie, Caroline Quentin) I have hopes that it could be an unthreatening commercial success. Judy has received some seed money to give us a new draft by the end of January.

I trust you may find the details of our work both relevant and of interest.

After Christmas, Frank wrote quibbling about the extent of the cut we had received, which we had put up on our website:

31st December 2011

Dear Frank,

Thank you for the correction about the figures. In fact, Graham and Jon Bradfield [Out of Joint's Marketing Manager] had not added in the Grants for the Arts Award [we had received an additional sum specifically for the training of an Associate Director. We selected a young graduate from Queen's University Belfast, Des Kennedy], but they had also counted the percentage cut from 2011/12 which all arts organisations received last year. Incidentally, the Grants for the Arts Award has been enormously beneficial. It may not have escaped your notice that two of Out of Joint's previous young directors who trained with the company gathered excellent reviews in 2011. Blanche McIntyre received huge praise for her productions of *Accolade* and, most recently, of *Foxfinder. Accolade* will be moving to the West End at some point in 2012. Jessica Swale was also much lauded for her production of an unknown Georgian play, *The Belle's Stratagem*, by Hannah Cowley. Both of them, as well as Des Kennedy, whose production of *How the World Began* had a successful run at the Arcola in November, are an addition to the pool of promising young directors, and I am very proud that Out of Joint has been instrumental in their training and education. All three of them, plus an earlier Associate, Naomi Jones, would be well capable of directing a future production for Out of Joint, should we ever be in a position to undertake more than a single production in the year. Training young directors creates an invaluable national resource. After all, Danny Boyle, who emerged as a director at the Royal Court during my artistic directorship there, is directing the opening ceremony of the Olympic Games! I think it's an aspect of Out of Joint's work which ACE must continue to invest in! At any rate, I will make sure the figures are corrected on our website. As you say, it does not alter the thrust of my argument.

Graham will have written up the Refreshed Business Model over Christmas and doubtless that will be on its way to you within the next couple of weeks. I'm sure it will help but it's not a magic trick: it's not going to conjure £130,000 or even £50,000 out of thin air.

Pardon me if I sound a bit weary. Yes of course we look forward to talking about the Strategic Touring Fund and the ACE Catalyst Tier 3 programme, but fundraising is a muddy path that Graham and I have plodded down before. Inevitably, every Conservative administration urges all arts organisations to raise money from the private and the commercial sectors. Historically this has been of limited success. In 1986 or 1987 the Royal Court raised a total of, I think, £22,000, with the help of matching funding from Joe Papp of The Public Theater, New York. However, in the following year both our donors and ourselves were exhausted and the sum raised barely reached £4,000.

We will certainly endeavour to raise money for a Commissioning Fund, and, in fact, I have already written to the Peggy Ramsay Foundation on this subject. Shortly before Christmas I received a letter from Laurence Harbottle saying he would raise our application at the January meeting but he didn't hold much hope of success. I will write to a further number of trusts and organisations as soon as possible. You offer support for assessing the value participants place on Out of Joint's work: 'If your Education Manager is interested, please tell him to get in touch.' In fact, our Education Manager is a 'her', and I will encourage Panda Cox to get in touch with you immediately.

You suggest that someone with fundraising expertise would be a valuable addition to the board. I think this is an admirable idea. I will certainly mention it at our next board meeting, which is on 12th January 2012 at 7 p.m. at Out of Joint. It would be excellent if you were able to attend this meeting. You would be made very welcome. Perhaps you could combine that with a visit to rehearsals in the afternoon?

Finally, you are kind enough to hope that doing simply one production this year will enable me to have a period of rest and revitalisation. Thank you. In 2006 I spent six months in hospital. Many people were very very lovely and supportive: my brother Nigel, Bill Gaskill, Graham Cowley and above all my then partner, now my wife, Stella Feehily. However, I longed to be back at work. Ironic though it may sound, I find work itself stimulating, regenerating and revitalising, and I can't help thinking that by in effect restricting me to a single production annually, the Arts Council is failing to make the best use of both my resources and Out of Joint's. However, if in a year's time we have developed two scripts ready to go into full rehearsal in 2013 and have the resources to undertake this work, we will have done very well.

Thank you for all your helpful suggestions and I look forward to the conversations you suggested. I will phone to arrange a time as soon as possible.

Best wishes for 2012.

PS. My letter had asked for a definition of 'participants' from whom ACE requires feedback. Your letter makes no mention of this, but doubtless your promised conversations with Panda Cox will reveal all.

The Arts Council had now become enthusiastic about collecting assessments both from members of the public and from 'participants': it seemed yet another evasion of responsibility. They didn't seem to trust their own judgement any more, let alone ours.

5th January 2012

Dear Frank,

Your assessment emphasises the necessity for feedback on the value of Out of Joint's work from 'participants'. Does this mean actors, production staff, artistic directors of theatres we visit, audiences, or all of the above? Obviously this information can be obtained, but to write to all the 'participants' will again take up a lot of time when I am about to go to Germany to conduct a highly paid workshop on Out of Joint's behalf and then I'm about to start re-rehearsing *Top Girls*. The response will invariably be excellent; why else would they write? Do the Arts Council really require this?

You may have noticed that in yesterday's *Guardian* Michael Billington commented on how theatre is 'living off its past' and how the main impact theatrically this year has been made by *Top Girls* (1981), *The Kitchen* (1959), *Saved* (1965), *Flare Path* (1942) and *Chicken Soup with Barley* (1956). I wrote to him making several points I've already made to you: that unless you find a star and of course a writer to author a piece that is a star vehicle, and then persuade them to tour (very unlikely), you are dependent on the past and the back catalogue: so *Top Girls* this year, *Our Country's Good* next. The 'subsidy per seat' pressure inevitably forces all companies to make conservative choices. A point I have already made to you.

And now a completely new matter. As you know, Out of Joint intend to visit the back catalogue and revive *Our Country's Good* in the autumn of 2012. However, Timberlake Wertenbaker, the author, is reluctant to let us have the rights. She feels irked and neglected by Out of Joint because we have already revived *Our Country's Good* once (in 1998), but we have not commissioned a play from her since *Break of Day* (1995). This feeling is shared by a number of writers; Caryl was initially unenthusiastic about reviving *Top Girls* and Mark Ravenhill will not allow us to do a further production of *Shopping and Fucking*. All of them want us to focus on new work, and do not wish to be simply defined by past glories. However, our commissioning budget for 2012/13 is already overcommitted, and of course has had to be cut back from the 2011/12 figure. We already have existing commissions out to Richard Bean (first draft already received), Nina Raine, Stella Feehily, Roy Williams, Rebecca Lenkiewicz, Robin Soans and Steve Waters. Commissioned work forms a vital, possibly the most vital, strand of Out of Joint's activities: eight out of Out of Joint's most recent ten productions have been commissioned plays. I am alarmed for the company's future if we are unable to develop new work, particularly from a writer with Timberlake's distinguished record.

So the question I want to put to you is this: Is there another 'pot' or fund you could suggest for this crucially important aspect of our work?

The answer came back swiftly this time. No: there were no further funds available for commissioning new work.

By the start of 2012, a number of things had become more apparent. The Arts Council had always made it clear that there was no appeal against their decision. They continued to proclaim it was an 'open and fair decision'. Yet there had been no consultation, not even a conversation; no appeal was allowed against a judgement made according to completely undeclared criteria. 'Open and fair' seemed not merely economical with the truth but a positive flaunting of their perversity. No 'cold spots', no further money for commissions, but renewed emphasis placed on 'a more efficient and revamped business plan'. My patience finally snapped once more after one further letter addressed to 'Dear Graeme' criticised a business model based on co-productions which had in fact accumulated reserves over the eighteen years of the company's existence that were predicted to be £439,000 at the end of the current financial year (2011/12). We had been offered a 'Clore Development Day', in which various Arts and ex-Arts Council folk would meet with the board and the management of Out of Joint to suggest a way forward. My most recent letter had ended on a relatively elegiac note. This was not a tone I would sustain long into the new year.

15th February 2012

Dear Frank,

As you must know from previous correspondence, Graham's name is not 'Graeme' but 'Graham'. This seems incredibly slipshod and casual. Perhaps yourself and some members of the Arts Council staff should attend a Clore Development Day in which you review the rudimentary protocol of addressing correspondence. I note that your email refers to not one of the points that Graham and I have brought up in recent emails and letters, namely the efficiency of the existing business plan; the impressive accumulated reserves; the consistency of the number of performance weeks per year; the resistance of actors to touring; and the difficulty of increasing fees from regional venues. I am eager to hear your thoughts on all these matters.

The four workshops I have done in the last three weeks will have earned Out of Joint £1,600. Even with the inevitable expenses deducted, the 'profit' will be well over £1,000. In Oxford a colleague of yours at the Arts Council, Richard, performed in the workshop with admirable commitment and considerable skill! He can tell you all. We are also investigating the possibility of setting up an inset day for teachers in the autumn, which could raise a 'profit' of £2,000 or so; a long-running literary workshop with Salisbury Playhouse, which will raise another £1,500; and a week-long devising workshop we are trialling with Oxford Playhouse, which should raise a further £1,000. I met Ian Rickson last week, who is keen to revive a 1997 Out of Joint production, *Blue Heart* by Caryl Churchill. I urged him to allow Out of Joint to form a consortium of producers to tour it. He wasn't keen. Apparently Juliet Stevenson has expressed enthusiasm for Caryl's work but she won't tour. Ian also recounted how depressed and disheartened his partner, Polly Teale, had become as a result of the total and equally inexplicable cut Shared Experience had suffered. I'm sure you must be aware of the inescapable feelings of worthlessness, impotence and guilt that afflict those who have suffered from your cuts. I was, however, delighted to see Polly is directing Helen Edmundson's new play *Mary Shelley*, which is coming shortly to the Oxford Playhouse. Does this mean Shared Experience are now in receipt of a Project Grant? Ian was also bitter and highly articulate about the tsunami of feelgood, undemanding theatre that pressure to increase box-office receipts has produced. In the face of *Singin' in the Rain*, *One Man, Two Guvnors* and *Noises Off* as well as jolly, rompalong productions of *The Recruiting Officer* and *She Stoops to Conquer*, it's hard to argue with his position. The Arts Council has to take a share of responsibility for this. At the least ACE should be encouraging companies that undertake a more serious and rigorous examination of our theatre history and heritage. I enclose a clipping from the *Guardian* which backs up this 'anecdotal' evidence [see Appendix 3].

I can't yet give you final attendance figures for our two weeks at the West Yorkshire Playhouse, but I am confident this will average over 200 and the advance in Exeter promises the same. [In the event, West Yorkshire Playhouse was 252, and Exeter was 439.] I look forward to your response to this letter and a more detailed response to my two earlier letters. Graham promises to finish the business plan next week and I will then seek to make an appointment with you.

At the same time, Graham made his own robust rebuttal:

20th February 2012

Dear Frank,

Max has shown me your emails of 15th and 17th February, in which you once again express support for the artistic work but cite the 'operation and business model' as the reasons you cut the grant. I've also seen your email to the board.

I know we've been talking about this in our various meetings, and I try to view the situation in as positive a light as I can. But I'm getting a bit tired of being endlessly beaten over the head with criticism of my business model. The truth is that our business model has worked very well, particularly since 2000/01, when the company was rewarded with a major uplift in funding by the Arts Council. In all that time the company has had a healthy surplus and, when deficits occurred in certain years, they were in each case a planned use of a portion of the reserves, and tightly controlled. The company started its life by co-producing, and this has remained our modus operandi ever since. It has given us a stability which is the envy of many companies. I have attached a table giving an overview of the last ten years, which might help.

What has rankled with me throughout this time is this: Had the Arts Council been concerned about our business model, why on earth did nobody mention it before? You have been our Drama Officer for years and years. Why didn't you mention it? Could it be because it wasn't a problem? The one mention I can recall is from Katy Griffiths' report of our Annual Review of 2009/10, when she thought we should be doing more fundraising. But why criticise us for not fundraising when there was no earthly reason to do so?

Your cut to our grant requires us to become more ingenious and 'use our assets' more effectively, to make up the shortfall that you have created. We will do it, but the fact is that it all takes an enormous amount of time and attention which, I firmly believe, would be better spent creating and supporting the work we are really here to do.

As well as diverting time and energy to 'using our assets', I also dedicated myself to collecting assessments of Out of Joint's work and delivering them to the Arts Council as urged. An earlier letter recounted the progress of *Top Girls*.

9th January 2012

Dear Frank,

Well, it's good to be back at work, and after three weeks' rehearsal *Top Girls* is looking remarkably good. Of course, it is one of the great plays of the twentieth century so there is that security although, between ourselves, I miss that thrill of uncertainty that accompanies new work. The big news is that plans to take *A Dish of Tea with Dr Johnson* to New York have crystallised in this last week, and it seems likely we may even go as early as April or May 2012. At the same time it's clear that transfers do not make Out of Joint's fortune: we made £3,093.75 from the run of *Top Girls* at Trafalgar Studios and £400 from *A Dish of Tea with Dr Johnson* at the Arts Theatre.

Our diminished programme of work for 2012/13 of course affects the whole theatre ecology, not simply those of us on the staff at Out of Joint. In 2011/12 we will have paid 510 actor-weeks; in 2012/13 Graham calculates this will fall to 327 weeks, and correspondingly design fees will also be lowered. Is this good for the recession?

I enclose five more letters of support. How many do you require? Our Education Manager, Panda Cox, attempted to contact you last week seeking advice about feedback from participants, but you were away. From what you have told me, the Arts Council don't seem very generous with their salary but they do seem remarkably magnanimous in their provision of leave! Barney Norris, my assistant, has been down to Salisbury and we hope to set up a scheme with the Playhouse whereby we provide support and expertise in play development. They are unable to afford even a part-time literary manager, and the idea is that we will run a programme to nurture and encourage a number of local writers. In the coming week I also have a

> meeting with the National Theatre Studio to quantify the
> amount of support they are able to give us in the coming year;
> Graham estimates that we have raised £9,000 from the
> University of Hertfordshire for the *Witches* project.

> My previous letter invited you to rehearsal and to the board
> meeting on the 12th of January. It would be good to know if
> this is a possibility for you.

*

Out of Joint had booked a two-month tour of *Top Girls* for the spring
of 2012. As I had feared, not one of the cast from the production in
Chichester and the subsequent run at the Trafalgar Studios wished to
tour. This was disappointing but not altogether surprising, as they had
been involved with the production for over three months already.
Actors are always falling in love with the next job on the horizon and
thereby slighting the present one! On these occasions, feelings of
betrayal and rage are unworthy and unjustified, but I had difficulty
suppressing them all the same. I did, however, save a week's re-
rehearsal by casting three of the understudies from the West End
production. They rose to the occasion splendidly, and saved me a lot
of time. We opened in Warwick in the middle of January (411 paying
punters per performance), where the audience was youthful and
enthusiastic. Theatres on university campuses, such as Exeter,
Southampton or Warwick, ironically often have difficulty in attracting student audiences, but this was an exception. Warwick was
followed by Oxford (407), Bury St Edmunds (187), Cheltenham
(233), Ipswich (345), Leeds (252) and Exeter (439). The figures were
perfectly satisfactory and in all but one case exceeded my self-
imposed target of two hundred paying punters per performance.
Satisfactory, but hardly overwhelming for a modern classic. The figures served to confirm rather than deny my hypothesis that the
regional audience for new work has declined substantially since 2005.
    It was high time to stop complaining and start work on something
new. At the beginning of February came the opportunity to work on

a completely fresh project. In part funded by the University of Hertfordshire and in part by the National Theatre Studio, I undertook a
two-week workshop on witches. The last woman to be convicted of
witchcraft in England was Jane Wenham in 1713. She came from the
small Hertfordshire village of Walkerne near Hertford. I do some regular teaching sessions at the University of Hertfordshire. The
proximity of Walkerne and the three hundredth anniversary of Jane
Wenham's conviction in 2013 had prompted the University of Hertfordshire to become involved. This unusual and intriguing
collaboration meant we had the invaluable advice and comprehensive
knowledge of Owen Davies as a constant presence in rehearsals.
Owen is the best kind of academic—thoughtful, enthusiastic and pos-
sessing a depth of knowledge which meant that within his field of
study he could provide detailed responses on almost any aspect of life
during that period. I have been fortunate to benefit from the expertise of many academics over the years, chief among them the great Roy
Foster of Hertford College, Oxford, and the best always upset the
donnish stereotype of the bookbound mind unwilling to venture outside their published opinions. The best academics know the most
unlikely things—Owen Davies could quote the price of bread in Suffolk in 1710 without a second thought, while Roy Foster could tell
you how many highway assassinations took place in Roscommon in
the 1880s more readily than most people can tell you the time. The
depth of knowledge possessed by writers like Owen and Roy, the
product of a life's enthusiasm, is a wonderful resource, and we took
profitable advantage from Owen's presence. The actors in the workshop were Robin Soans, Lisa Kerr, Jack Farthing, Franc (Frances)
Ashman and Lucy Briers, all of whom I had worked with on a number of previous projects, Nick Lee and Susan Engel, both of whom I
had met socially, and Alexis Zegerman, who was then working at the
National Theatre. Together they formed an enthusiastic and zestful
company, and with Owen's guidance we accumulated a great deal of
expertise on eighteenth-century witchcraft during the two-week
workshop. An early expedition organised by Stephanie Grainger of

the University of Hertfordshire took us to the pretty village of Walk-erne. In February there had been a heavy snowfall, and the village looked like an English Christmas card. In the lane opposite the church were a number of well-maintained and picturesque cottages. The one where Jane Wenham had lived was helpfully called Witch's Cottage. 'If only she had hung on for another three centuries, she could have sold this for £500,000,' said one of the actors cheerfully. Jane had been accused of laying a spell on one of the servants at the vicarage, who had a series of epileptic fits. The beautiful Queen Anne vicarage (£1,500,000) was situated three hundred yards away across a field.

Back at the National Theatre Studio and for two days at the theatre on the University of Hertfordshire's Hatfield campus, we began a series of improvisations. To begin with these were inevitably shallow, reflecting our limited knowledge, but over the two weeks they became more and more pertinent. I decided to capitalise on the actors' great skill at developing characters, asking each of the actors to assume a particular role within the village community that we created. Lisa Kerr and Nick Lee became tenant farmers, Aoife and Fergal McGuire, newly immigrated from County Monaghan. Robin was Francis Hutchinson, Bishop of Down and Connor and their landlord, a real figure who had been a young vicar in Bury St Edmunds at the height of the East Anglian witch hunts led by Matthew Hopkins fifty years earlier. Hutchinson was an informed and influential sceptic who in 1711 published a pamphlet dismissing the long-held and superstitious signs by which a witch could be identified. We thought of our improvisations as taking place in 1713. Franc Ashman invented a role as a baby farmer who took in a number of infants whose parents in London either did not want to acknowledge them or who were thought to benefit from the country air. Alexis was a widow who ran an unlicensed beer parlour in the front room of her cottage. This brought her into conflict with the bishop, who was the major landlord of the area. Susan was 'a cunning woman' who possessed particular knowledge of herbs and plants and who acted as the local vet. Jack was playing the vicar who had just graduated from Emmanuel College,

Cambridge, and who had recently been appointed to the living. Emmanuel was known at this time to produce graduates who held particularly low church and puritanical views.

Now we had the characters I was able to set up various situations which put them under particular pressure. First of all Nick Lee as Fergal McGuire put his sheep into a low-lying, swampy meadow where they developed splay foot. Susan Engel was blamed, and Robin, doubling as a particularly obstreperous and elderly ram, escaped into the corridor of the studio and bleated his way into the Green Room, to the puzzlement of actors from other workshops drinking coffee there. Franc also doubled as the bishop's house-keeper, and there was clear evidence of a romantic attachment between them, much to the dismay of the bishop's long-suffering wife, Lucy Briers. The newly appointed vicar, Jack, was asked by the bishop to suppress Alexis's beer parlour, but his task was made more difficult by the romantic liaison he had formed with Alexis's merry widow. Disaster struck the village as one of Franc's infants died of a mysterious fever, and Lisa and Nick's much-desired child was still-born. This occurred during a particularly difficult lambing season, when both parents were up all night delivering lambs. Lucy quali-fied for the prestigious award of 'Most Promising Pregnant Ewe'.

In one particularly poignant improvisation, the boys were dis-patched to the Green Room while one of the girls was selected at random to take her clothes off and submit to an examination by the other women to see whether they could find identifying marks of witchcraft. Rebecca, our author, herself drew the unlucky card and sportingly stripped off to be examined by the other women. Their shrieks of horror reached us in the Green Room as they discovered that Rebecca was certainly a witch. We also found a possible title, *Rough Music*. This was the cacophony of fearsome noise made with pots, pans and agricultural instruments used to harass a suspected witch and drive her from the village.

In January I was also re-rehearsing *Top Girls* for its Out of Joint tour.

16th January 2012

Dear Frank,

I'm sorry you couldn't make it to rehearsal or to the board meeting, but the good news is that *Top Girls* looks in tremendous shape. Caryl saw a run yesterday and was very pleased. As you know, it is an entirely new cast, although I have used three of the understudies from the Trafalgar Studios. This is another example of Out of Joint giving opportunities to young people, and I am especially pleased and proud that this has worked out so well. The advances continue to build steadily, although Bury St Edmunds is a bit slow. Less good news is my meeting with Laura Collier at the National Theatre Studio. They will of course help us with the *Witches* project as they have already undertaken. They are likely to support us with *This May Hurt A Bit*, subject to scrutiny of the script at the end of March. They will also consider a week's workshop in June 2012 for the verbatim Gareth Thomas project. [The small Welsh town of Bridgend, fifteen miles from Cardiff, was the home of the Welsh rugby star, Gareth Thomas, who had come out as gay in 2009. The town had also had an 'epidemic' of teenage suicides in 2006 which had caught the attention of the press, who speculated (inaccurately) that some secret suicide cult was involved. The idea was for a verbatim play which might link these two stories together.] But they are unable to help in any way with *Pitcairn*, Richard Bean's dystopia about the ultimate fate of the *Bounty* mutineers. This is bad news as the play has at the moment a cast of nineteen, which would of course be beyond our resources in any year, and one of the purposes of a workshop would be to find a way to condense the material. That is also a joint commission with the National Theatre, although Nick Hytner doesn't care for the play and won't take it further. The play is now with Michael Boyd at the RSC and Jonathan Church at Chichester. I look forward to updating you on all these projects when we meet.

Thank you for responding to Trudie Styler so swiftly and for advising Panda Cox about feedback procedures. [A number of actors had written to the Arts Council on our behalf following our cut, and it had become clear that ACE were growing weary of the correspondence. The latest supplicant on our behalf had been Trudie Styler, following her run in *A Dish of Tea with Dr Johnson.*] However, I note that you still take consolation in ACE's decision being a 'fair and open' process. This defies logic. I ask once again, what is 'fair and open' about a decision taken behind closed doors, with no consultation, no appeal, and judged by criteria to which there had been no previous reference? I also had a rather tetchy letter from George Darling [Frank Endwright's colleague at the Arts Council] last week. He appeared irritated by the number of feedback letters urging the Arts Council to reconsider their decision. He pointed out that you had ruled this out at our meeting last year. I am well aware of this, but can hardly be held responsible if the arcane and baffling procedures and decisions of the Arts Council are not fully understood by our supporters. You have been urging us to give you feedback, and indeed it must be clear to you by now that your decision to reduce Out of Joint's NPO [National Portfolio Organisation] funding has dismayed people from all sections of the theatre community. I look forward to sending you the responses of the *Top Girls* 'participants'.

At the board meeting, Iain Gillie, the Executive Director of the Curve, Leicester, substantiated the anecdotal evidence I have already given you, about the difficulty of obtaining and sustaining audiences for drama in the regions. At the Curve, *As You Like It* played to 23%, *All My Sons* to 27% and *One Flew Over the Cuckoo's Nest*, hardly a 'threatening' choice, to 38%. Under these circumstances, he felt *Bang Bang Bang* had performed satisfactorily and he attributed the rather larger audiences we got for *Mixed Up North* to the amount of education workshops that that particular show attracted. John Blackmore [then Executive Director at Bolton Octagon, and the Chairman of the Board of Out of Joint] concurred with these opinions, and said there was a downward trend in subscription bookers in Bolton, who were now far more selective and conservative in their choices.

I enclose the script of *Pitcairn*, which I look forward to discussing when we meet.

Post-Christmas, our correspondence had embraced a less formal and more friendly tone. I didn't consider that this was a change of great significance; it was perhaps more a weary acknowledgment that we were to be yoked together for a good few furlongs. However, it was also becoming clear within the limited means at his disposal that Frank was inclined to help us, and did not wish to see Out of Joint perish. This at least was a small step forward.

24th January 2012

Dear Frank,

Thank you for your courteous response to my earlier letter which I have received but haven't had time to study properly. The next board meeting has been arranged for 2nd February and has been called specifically to discuss the composition and function of the board, and to debate various issues which your colleagues at ACE have raised. Your presence would be very useful, and you would be made very welcome.

Top Girls opened at the Warwick Arts Centre last week, and although the final figures are not yet available I think it will be near 400 paying punters per night, which will I think exceed our previous record (340 for Caryl's *Blue Heart*) at Warwick. Of course, we have no control over the pricing policies of the venues we visit, but it was particularly striking how many students and young people attended last week.

The fact that *Top Girls* is widely studied in colleges and schools is obviously a huge help. But while it is appropriate to celebrate this success, it is also sobering to think that reviving past successes is not a long-term option for Out of Joint. *Our Country's Good* next, yes, but then? Mark Ravenhill has no wish for us to revive *Shopping and Fucking,* and I wouldn't wish to essay *The Steward of Christendom* again without Donal McCann. And if we create no new plays what will our successors revive in thirty years' or one hundred and thirty years' time? The history of eighteenth-century theatre is a salutary lesson here. Throughout the eighteenth century, market forces made the theatres bigger and bigger, and managers became increasingly reluctant to produce new work. Why risk poor houses with a new play when it was much safer to revive a Shakespeare or a Beaumont and Fletcher? Consequently only Sheridan and Goldsmith survive from this period, and both of them began their careers in Dublin, where theatre remained 'middle scale'.

The response to *Top Girls* at the first post-show discussion was notably enthusiastic, but there were exceptions. There were three ladies in the front row who clearly wished the play had been more of a trenchant anti-Thatcher polemic. They thought the women should be more angry, more 'polarised'. It transpired that one of them had been the director of a theatre company aimed at children with learning difficulties which had had its funding completely withdrawn in the last round of cuts. At once I understood their anger, and I also remembered the point you and George had made when we met last year: that there were companies like the Almeida or Shared Experience who had suffered yet more than Out of Joint.

The value of training an Associate Director was also brought home to me last week. Des Kennedy took two excellent and much-appreciated workshops with local schools, so after the first performance I felt able to return to London confident that he was well capable of watching the show and giving notes for the rest of the week. Incidentally our income from education work will have more than doubled in the current year. In 2010/11 this was £1,725 while estimates for the current year are that it is likely to be in excess of £5,250.

Graham has found that drafting the business plan is taking longer than anticipated but is working on it. I do hope you can come to the meeting on 2nd February.

PS. 'Friends' now stand at 28 with over £4,400 raised from these sources, but we have received confirmation that the Peggy Ramsay Foundation are unable to help us. We are now applying to several other trusts and foundations and are awaiting their response.

Whenever I work in the United States I'm reminded how important it is to train young directors. In September 2007 I directed J.T. Rogers' *The Overwhelming* for the Roundabout Theatre in New York; however, I wasn't long out of hospital, and in the course of rehearsal I had a relapse, later diagnosed as an episode of Transient Global Amnesia, and had five very comfortable but extremely expensive days in the Cornell Presbyterian Hospital. I was absent from rehearsal for ten days, during which time my excellent Assistant Director Jojo Groenhuit assumed full responsibility and directed the play with great verve and confidence. Despite her vital role, the Roundabout declined to give her any billing in the programme. When I pressed her case I was simply told it wasn't their policy to credit assistants. I imagine that if they had done so, it would have triggered some mandatory Equity payment they were anxious to avoid.

Instead, the role of rehearsing a new actor is customarily taken by the stage manager, who becomes a kind of répétiteur, mimicking the exact movements of the original actor—saying, for example, 'No, you stand and *then* you pick up the coffee cup.' This addresses neither motivation nor the emotional state for the poor actor, and I have several times returned to New York to find that actors have been replaced and that my production has become a hollow fragment of its former splendour. In Russia, of course, their system is even more impressive than ours; every directing graduate from drama school would be offered two years' work as an assistant in a major company.

26th January 2012

Dear Max,

Thank you for your email. I'm delighted that *Top Girls* is doing so well. It is striking how students/young people attended in Warwick but not in Exeter, Southampton, etc.; this may of course be something to do with the relationship that Warwick Arts Centre has with its students. I'm afraid I don't have much hard information about the attendance of young people regionally; anecdotally, these are holding up in London.

You may have seen the headline in last week's *Stage* about falling regional audiences. These were based on info from Regularly Funded Organisation submissions 2010/11 (so doesn't include commercial theatres) [Regularly Funded Organisations were rechristened National Portfolio Organisations in 2011]. If you didn't realise, this document is published on our website.

As you can see from the tables I've copied from it, total audiences for (subsidised) theatre have fallen – although the total number of performances fell slightly at the same time.

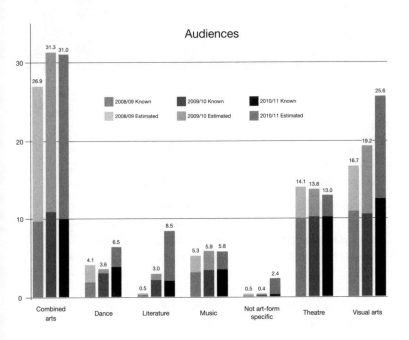

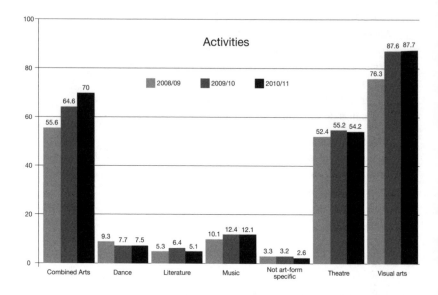

This would seem to further support our joint observations that it has become harder to attract audiences. Hopefully (as I've said before), our Strategic Touring Fund, which is an attempt to support audience development, will help with this issue.

I agree with your historical analysis of the eighteenth-century theatre and would add that the early nineties felt like they were a not dissimilar period – my memory is of a lot of *Shirley Valentines* on offer…! As for the current state of affairs, in fact, 73% of the portfolio commissioned at least one new work – which feels to me like that is very different to the early nineties, or indeed the eighteenth century! Not that we should in any way be complacent – since, despite there being more new commissions presented in '10/11 than the previous year, these were still less than in the year before that.

I shall be attending the board meeting on Thurs 2nd – can you tell me what time it starts?

See you next week.

30th January 2012

Dear Frank,

Thank you for your letter. I am delighted you will be able to come to the board meeting, which is at 7 p.m. on the 2nd February. It will be very helpful. In Oxford last week, where there were 514 in on Tuesday night. I wasn't totally happy with the performance, however; certainly the actors have grown in confidence after a week's playing, but some of the detail of the rehearsal room had been lost and had not yet been compensated for by the energy of the performance. I blame myself in part; the Oxford Playhouse has quite difficult acoustics with an overhanging balcony, and the simultaneous dialogue of the first scene must have been particularly difficult to follow. The two-hour technical rehearsal was insufficient time to deal with this, nor did I allow enough time for a detailed note session afterwards, and hasty, whispered notes prior to the post-show discussion were probably not particularly helpful. A full notes session the next day would have necessitated the expense of an extra night's stay. So of course I saved the money.

Thank you for your advice about the feedback forms which were circulated in both Warwick and Oxford. I was, however, puzzled to learn from Jon Bradfield, our Marketing Manager, that you have no wish for us to forward the forms to you and that they are for our own benefit and edification. I was totally taken aback; it may seem arrogant but after 46 years in the theatre I feel I know how we're doing without additional information. I wrote to you that it takes six months after the conclusion of a particular production to regain some objectivity. So I can write now that the author, Stephen Jeffreys', absence in Hollywood meant we were always two drafts behind where we might have been with *The Convict's Opera*. I can see that *Andersen's English* may have done better to focus more on Catherine Dickens rather than the better-known figure of Charles. And yes, I can see that while *Bang Bang Bang* was never going to be about the Congolese any more than *Our Country's Good* is about the Aboriginals, it would have been good to have had a further scene about Colonel Mburame, because he was such a fascinating character.

I know that *Top Girls* is being received enthusiastically and that the production is, if anything, an improvement on the one this summer at Chichester. I also know it wasn't at its very best last week in Oxford, and I look forward to getting my hands on it this week in Bury St Edmunds. I also know that after thirty years the play still divides people because of the provocative structure. There were many warm comments on the Warwick Arts Centre website, but there was also: 'Abysmal. Simply the worst play I have ever seen in my life.' What am I to do about that? Suicide or immediate resignation seems the only valid response, and I intend to essay neither!

I know that what audiences really want is Comedy, Sex, Frocks, Satire and perhaps a small soupçon of political provocation. I also know that though Out of Joint occasionally purveys one of these ingredients, quite often we don't. I can point to *Shopping and Fucking* (Sex), *Feelgood* (Satire and Comedy), *Andersen's English* (Frocks) but also to *Flight Path*, *Testing the Echo*, *A State Affair* and *Mixed Up North,* which had few of these ingredients, but all are productions of which I remain immensely proud.

So I look forward to a conversation when you reveal the pertinence and purpose of these feedback forms. My attempt to persuade Patrick Marber to take on *Love and a Bottle* failed. I shall have to think again, but Stella Feehily has delivered the first half of her new play about the NHS, and Judy Upton has delivered a new draft of *Gaby Goes Global* which I am about to read.

7th February 2012

Dear Frank,

Thank you so much for coming to the board meeting last week. All of us found it very helpful. *Top Girls* continues to do well. I thought the show looked good on the Bury St Edmunds stage and my prediction of about 170 paying punters per night will, I think, be fairly accurate. [It was 187.] Still, this is about 70 paying punters per night fewer than I would have anticipated five years ago. The reviews and the feedback continue to be broadly favourable, although they have swung from 'It was a mistake to revive a play that was so much a product of its time' to 'Definitely still as relevant today, now we've got the fucking Tories back'. I have attached comments positive and negative.

As you heard at the board meeting, *A Dish of Tea with Dr Johnson* has been postponed. [Allan Buchman of Culture Project in New York had stated he didn't have the funding for *A Dish of Tea with Dr Johnson* and *The Seagull* as well. Later it was to transpire that he didn't have the funding for that either.] The producer has assured us of his enthusiasm for programming the play next year when he has opened his theatre and raised more money. One interesting sideline to this is that the producer (Allan Buchman) is looking for an artistic director and has made preliminary soundings as to my availability and enthusiasm. Whether this would be a full-time or consultative post is not yet clear. I have been offered jobs in America before – in the mid-eighties Joseph Papp asked me if I would be interested in succeeding him at The Public Theater, but I was very much involved with the Royal Court at the time. About ten years later I was asked if I wanted to be one of a triumvirate of directors running the Shakespeare Festival in Stratford, Ontario. I have always seen my career as being in this country, reflecting and commenting on our own society, but on these previous occasions I have also been confident about the Arts Council's support. As you may have gathered at the board meeting, there is a certain level of paranoia that rightly or wrongly is the current perception at Out of Joint from the board through the whole staff about our relationship with ACE. The huge cut and the questions about governance, which I assure you we have every intention of addressing, have made us feel out of favour and picked on. As you will doubtless have gathered from the many letters of support, your decision has surprised and shocked the theatre world at all levels. Clearly it would be unfair to ask you to predict the Arts Council's decision about the next round of funding in two-and-a-half years' time, however, this is likely to be the last chance I get to make a start elsewhere, and if I felt Out of Joint was unlikely to regain the sunshine of the Arts Council smile I would welcome a quiet word. If it's likely that Out of Joint will only be able to produce one play a year I would be tempted to go somewhere I could be more fully involved.

Gaby Goes Global looks promising but needs more work, and the same is true of *This May Hurt A Bit*.

I didn't anticipate that Frank would be able to respond to my directness, but I think he went as far as he was able in his next letter.

14th February 2012

Dear Max,

Thank you for your letter of 7th February and also thank you for inviting me to the board meeting.

I'm glad that *Top Girls* continues to thrive, albeit to smaller audiences than you would have predicted for it for five years ago. My personal feeling is (as I am sure you would agree) that polarised reviews and feedback are much preferable to a uniformity of lukewarm-ness.

At the board meeting I had detected a degree of paranoia directed at the Arts Council. Perhaps I can use this opportunity to clarify some things starting with governance. As an organisation we have detailed knowledge of about 700 or so arts organisations and their boards, and I can assure you that any similar manifestations of issues relating to governance (some of which were characterised as being grounds for 'serious concern' by your own auditors) would – and are – met with a similar sort of response. [In March 2010 my mortgage had expired, and RBS had declined to offer a renewal on the grounds of my age. I borrowed £50,000 from Out of Joint, promising to pay it back within two years. In fact, the debt was repaid by January 2012, but the Arts Council looked askance at this arrangement, even though the money was borrowed from our now legendary and, in their eyes, overinflated reserves.] In that context I would draw your attention to the

Clore board-development programme for organisations that we regularly fund.

Secondly, can I reiterate that we have the highest regard for the artistic work of Out of Joint generally and, of course, your own work in particular. Our decision to award a level of funding lower than your RFO grant [RFO = Regularly Funded Organisation. The change of acronym from 'RFO' to 'NPO' – National Portfolio Organisation – had occurred at the same time as our cut. I don't know whether this implied a lessening of commitment, but the Arts Council's language was canny and slippery. 'Investment' had replaced 'funding' at some time in the eighties.] was never related to our view of the work, and I believe if you look back at our correspondence you will see that we have had nothing but praise for the work itself. Our reasons for the lower grant award were entirely to do with the operation and business model of Out of Joint.

It is in our shared interest that our effort supports the artistic work of the company in the best way we can, and it seems to me that Out of Joint should be able to become a stronger and more productive organisation which is better able to support you as an artist to create and develop the work that you would like. We have previously discussed with you some of the areas that we think the organisation would benefit from considering – from a more effective production model to better use of company assets – and we are pleased that Graham's outline of the forthcoming business plan touched upon some of these areas.

Lastly, I am not surprised that you have been sounded out for a prestigious job overseas; as you say, this is not the first time. Your ability to find and develop plays that look at our society is recognised and admired by all. I think everyone in the theatre world – including the Arts Council – would be deeply saddened if you choose to pursue your work abroad.

Of course no one can predict what will happen in two-and-a-half years' time; however, at the moment your current Programme of Activity (i.e. what we fund Out of Joint to do for the next three years) states that after next year's revival of *Our Country's Good*, Out of Joint intends to produce two new plays a year. You will have a lot of things to consider when making your choices; however, I believe that Out of Joint will remain as an option that provides you with the infrastructure and support you would like – and we sincerely hope that that is the route you choose.

In the next letter I attempted to give Frank an account of our *Witches* workshop which had just concluded.

15th February 2012

Dear Frank,

Top Girls continues to do well. We were at Cheltenham this last week, although the cast felt the rather conservative Cheltenham audience were resistant to both the form and political content of the play. In London we completed our first week of the workshop on witches with Rebecca Lenkiewicz. Owen Davies, senior lecturer in History at the University of Hertfordshire, has been in attendance and has been of tremendous help. There isn't much the cast of eight now don't know about eighteenth-century witchcraft. They have developed various characters and storylines, some based on real historical characters and real events. It's been fascinating, but of course the only true measure of success is whether it will stimulate Rebecca Lenkiewicz to write a play. Meanwhile, back at the office, Panda Cox, has been estimating our 'subsidy per seat' ratio for the current year. With a few weeks still to go to the end of the financial year it promises to be somewhere between £8 and £9, a considerable difference from the £15 you quoted us for last year. But I have severe reservations about 'subsidy per seat' being a valid measurement of worth. *A Dish of Tea with Dr Johnson* played in a number of small theatres and arts centres. By most criteria it was a success and played to high percentages, but the limited capacity of the various theatres would make the subsidy per seat remarkably high for this particular production. This measurement, if insisted upon, will inevitably drive companies to make more timid, conventional and conservative programming choices. Surely the Arts Council was founded to reverse this tendency?

I must also report that we're in some difficulty with Richard Bean's *Pitcairn*. As the first draft stands it requires a cast of nineteen. Clearly this is beyond the resources of anybody but the big national companies. Both Chichester and the RSC have shown interest in the project, and both may well host a reading in order to test the material. I feel we need a rather longer development period, both to contextualise the remarkable story in the world of the eighteenth century, and to endeavour to shrink the cast size. But Richard Bean fears 'interference', I think, and is certainly reluctant to reduce the cast size. We're at an impasse. Have you had a chance to read the script I sent you?

Given the healthy level of Out of Joint's reserves, which continued to rise in 2011/12, the suggestion that the cut in our funding was 'entirely due to the operation and business model of Out of Joint' seems an evasion. As George Darling was later to admit, the Arts Council was looking for the maximum cuts that any company could endure. In this context, the existence of our £400,000 of reserves was clearly a liability. We may have been hoist by our own prudence and good housekeeping!

17th February 2012

Dear Max,

Thank you for the update.

As I have said before, our concerns are to do with the operation and business model of Out of Joint. These relate to many different aspects – including the high level of overheads you have and the low levels of income generated, the low level of performances, the low [sic] levels of subsidy per performance and (yes) per audience compared with peers. I know that 'subsidy per seat' has occupied your thoughts, but I would like to state again that this is one indicator only and they are all tied together.

I have passed *Pitcairn* to a colleague who has had experience as a reader for a number of producing outfits. However, it is not really our job to comment on drafts nor (I think, you would agree) should it be.

At this point we had begun negotiations with Culture Project in New York to bring over our production of *A Dish of Tea with Dr Johnson*, and also for me to direct a reading of *The Seagull*.

20th February 2012

Dear Frank,

Thank you for your reply of 15th February. Clearly you can't predict the Arts Council's response to Out of Joint's funding application in three years' time, but I found the reassurance contained in your letter very helpful. Although *A Dish of Tea with Dr Johnson* has been postponed till 2013 it appears the workshop on *The Seagull* which was to accompany it will still go ahead. The financial model for this has not yet been finalised, but it could be an additional source of income for Out of Joint.

The number of paying punters per night was 233 in Cheltenham for *Top Girls*. The cast then took a well-deserved holiday week, while I finished the workshop on *Witches* at the National Theatre Studio. The Studio is an incredible resource, and it has been a real privilege to work with such a diverse and talented group of actors over this time. They combined together wonderfully and together with our tame academic, Owen Davies, they have provided Rebecca Lenkiewicz with an extraordinary body of information and material. One of the real-life figures we learnt about was Francis Hutchinson, Bishop of Down and Connor, who wrote what most academics regard as the definitive contemporary dismissal of witchcraft in 1711. As a young vicar in Bury St Edmunds, he had become involved in the case of John Lowes, vicar of Brandeston, who unwisely gave shelter to a woman accused of witchcraft in his vicarage. He was then accused of being a witch himself by his angry parishioners and after two trials was hung in the Market Square, Bury St Edmunds, in 1656. I was intrigued to read in the *Guardian Guide* on Saturday that Eastern Angles, who are touring their new play, *Private Resistance*, to village halls in Suffolk and Norfolk, are actually performing in Brandeston Village Hall as well as in Woodbridge, Wivenhoe and Framlingham. All these villages and market towns were visited by Matthew Hopkins, the Witchfinder General, and in all of them he discovered witches. It would be tremendously exciting to emulate Eastern Angles and take Rebecca's play to the same villages. It would of course mean that we would have to limit our ambitions with the set and lighting, and it would mean getting extra revenue to supplement the doubtless very small box-office income. But surely these are 'cold spots'. The temperature was, after all, -11° in Bury St Edmunds when we were there a few weeks ago!

You now point to Out of Joint's business model as a reason behind the cut – however, it is a business model that has served the company spectacularly well for twenty years. We are taking forward accumulated reserves of over £400,000 at the end of the financial year. This is an increase of some £48,000 on the accumulated reserves of 2010/11 and comes in a year when the company, along with all other arts institutions, has suffered a 6.7% cut and has in addition produced 3 successful shows. Not much wrong with the business model here!

I understand from Graham that the Clore Development Day has been fixed for 21st May after my planned return from New York. I look forward to it.

I never got a response to my suggestion that we might tour to villages and towns in East Anglia, but, as I write in April 2013, we have had a productive meeting with Ivan Cutting, the director of Eastern Angles, and our current intention is to spend two weeks of Out of

Joint's spring 2015 tour going to those same villages in Suffolk where Matthew Hopkins 'discovered' witches. Rebecca Lenkiewicz is due to deliver a revised draft of the Witches play, now called *Rough Music* in May 2013.

5th March 2012

Dear Frank,

The confirmed attendance figure for *Top Girls* at Bury St Edmunds was 187 paying punters per night, just below our self-appointed target of 200, whereas Cheltenham was 233, just above. The tour continues for the next two weeks in Leeds before our final week in Exeter. Workshop activity has been intense with several teams of workshop leaders darting up and down the country – it sometimes seems that Out of Joint are subsidising British Rail. I did one in York on Wednesday and a three-hour one in Leicester yesterday. The fees for these occasions vary wildly. We have £800 from Cambridge, £700 from Lincoln, £500 from York and Leicester, but Exeter prevaricated for two months before finally agreeing to £300 making it a total of £2,800. All academic institutions are undoubtedly very budget-conscious, and we may have reached our income ceiling here.

You may have seen that I became involved by way of a *Guardian* blog with the debate that the Simon Stephens interview for Theatrevoice provoked. I enclose my 'comment' [see Appendix 3] and the responses that subsequently accrued, including George's desperate and futile attempt at reassurance today. Your most recent letter says you know that 'subsidy per seat has occupied your thoughts, but that this is one indicator only and they are all tied together'. A neutral observer might feel that having as it were kicked 'subsidy per seat' into the long grass you are now raising the other indicators in a futile attempt to justify your unjustifiable and iniquitous decision. But no matter; let us examine the new points you raise. High overheads: this is indeed a grievous fault and grievously has Out of Joint answered it. In Graham's budget for 2012/13 overheads have been reduced by £33,185 or 9.2%. Voluntary pay cuts have been taken by Graham and me; staffing departures have given us an opportunity to restructure staff internally. What we can't do is operate with fewer staff. When we have a production on tour, our five permanent staff and two part-time staff are severely overstretched. The next point you mention is 'the low level of income generated'. Of course our business plan seeks to maximise that. I'm sure it's unnecessary to point out that in the future our income will be less because we will be able to tour less.

Next you mention 'low level of performances'. I find this both baffling and devious. Touring weeks have been remarkably consistent over Out of Joint's history. In 1998 there was a spike when we undertook a commercial tour of *Shopping and Fucking*, and in 2007 it dipped to eight weeks when I was in hospital for six months. The last five years have been 11, 24, 13, 20 and 20 respectively, or an average of 17 weeks per year. I recall mentioning the number of touring weeks to you in one of the annual assessments during your first incarnation as Out of Joint's Relationship Manager. Not in 20 years has any member of the Arts Council expressed it as a concern. Of course we would like to tour each production more. There are two factors that prevent this. The first is that the venues themselves have been so squeezed financially that the fees we receive have barely increased in eighteen years; consequently each touring week does not cover its costs and is a drain on our reserves. The other factor is the actors' own tolerance for touring. A tour which involves more than eight weeks out of London, where almost all actors are based, becomes a disincentive. Relationships, schooling, pets, medical appointments, regular gym sessions and the inability to undertake voice-overs have all been offered as cogent and potent reasons for actors not to tour. Caroline Catz was only able to tour with *Top Girls* because the single holiday week which Graham had factored in coincided with half-term (she has two small children of school age). However, Graham has been able to obtain somewhat increased fees for both *Top Girls* and *Our Country's Good*. The planned tour of the latter is now thirteen weeks, which includes weeks in both Aberystwyth and the Hague. It goes without saying that neither such enhanced fees nor such a lengthy tour would be possible with new, more 'threatening' work. In this case I mean 'threatening' to venues. As you probably know, many of our productions depend for their quality on senior actors who have this varied range of domestic issues, which is why in the past it has been our practice to pay slightly above the touring allowance. This is no longer possible, and I fear that inevitably the quality and depth of our acting talent will be denied to us.

You mention 'low level of subsidy per performance', but I think you mean 'high levels'. We have already covered that. Finally, you write 'low level of performance and (yes) per audience compared with peers'. This is the hardest indicator to refute, because you have the facts and I don't, but it is also the hardest for you to assert. You cannot simply compare company with company. Of course some shows by some other companies have done better than some Out of Joint shows, but I would think any company's production of more 'threatening' new work matches our own experience. It is as tedious for me to repeat these arguments as, doubtless, it is for you to read them, but, as Billington's article last Christmas detailed, most people go to the theatre to see a particular actor and a particular performance. In the early eighties the Royal Court presented a season of Howard Brenton's work. There were two new plays, both of which got a series of what would now be called three-star reviews. The difference in attendance between the two plays was, however, marked. The one that had Diana Rigg played to 100 more paying punters per night than the other. The presence of Paula Wilcox in our production of Stella Feehily's *Dreams of Violence* probably brought in 30 people a night and Caroline Catz in *Top Girls* probably pulls in 20. Any valid comparisons must compare like with like as nearly as possible. I dare say *Top Girls* is performing as well as any straight drama on tour at the moment. *The Big Fellah* and *One Man, Two Guvnors* are of course by the same writer, but were the latter to tour, as doubtless it will, it would of course pack out, whereas *The Big Fellah*, alas, did not. You have to factor in the kind of drama each company is presenting, and then I would be fascinated to have a detailed conversation about comparison with our peers. [The conversation never took place.]

But if you wish to compare us with our peers, I don't believe any peer company show either both our commitment to generating and producing new plays from a whole range of writing experience or have the determination to hold the mirror up to our own society and reflect and comment upon the problems, perplexities and potentials of our time in a potent, provocative, theatrical and purposeful manner.

Like you I am eager to move on and discuss the future, but, alas, the decision you have taken in the immediate past circumscribes and limits our present and our future so comprehensively that we must refer to the past and attempt to learn from it.

In a subsequent meeting following my return from the US, George Darling conceded that the number of performance weeks was not a factor. However, with one production in 2012/13 our touring weeks were down to eleven, which equalled the lowest in any year of Out of Joint's existence and, of course, the first year ever with no new play.

*

And then in April 2012 I did something completely different. I had accepted the invitation to go to New York to do a three-week rehearsal for a reading of *The Seagull*. I had been asked to suggest a Chekhov play that interested me and my mind had circled back to the rather extraordinary adaptation of *The Seagull* by Thomas Kilroy, which he had done for me at the Royal Court and which set the play not in Russia but in County Galway in 1886. I had directed it in 1981 with Alan Rickman, Anna Massey, Harriet Walter and T.P. McKenna. It was time to visit it again, so on 18th April 2012, Stella and I flew to New York, appropriately enough via Dublin. For six weeks I could put the perfidious and unwarranted behaviour of the Arts Council behind me.

New York never fails to be a fascinating city to work in. My first acquaintance had been in 1959 when I got an exchange scholarship to Riverdale Country Day School at 242nd Street and Fieldston Road in the Bronx. It was a very different experience to my English public school. To start with, there were girls; and the abiding social anxiety was who to take to the Cerebral Palsy Ball. There was one boarding house, but supervision was liberal, and at the weekends I would take the subway down to the Village to go to the theatre Off-Broadway. I saw a legendary production of *The Balcony* and the first ever production of Edward Albee's *Zoo Story*, as well as an influential Living Newspaper production. These visits were my first real immersion in theatre since my annual fascination with pantomimes that my grandmother used to take me to; always one at the Lewisham Hippodrome, and one in the West End.

It was 1969 before I visited New York again, this time to direct *Dear Janet Rosenberg, Dear Mr Kooning* by Stanley Eveling, which had been a big success both in London and in Edinburgh. In New York I was working for the Hal Prince Organisation. There was some idea of casting Hume Cronyn in the role. This came to nothing but I had a very civilised lunch with him in The Algonquin. After I had cast the play it was cheaper for the Hal Prince Organisation to keep me in New York for the five weeks before rehearsals started rather than send me back to London. I had to go on the overnight sleeper to Toronto to have my visa validated, which was a lovely adventure, but apart from that it was a lonely time. I knew nobody. However, Stanley's play was splendidly seaworthy and it survived my rather sophomoric direction, got a great review in the *New York Times* and ran for a decent period. Immediately, my life in New York was transformed. The phone never stopped ringing, and girls I had casually met once rang to ask whether I was interested in going out 'for cocktails'. My dates included a stunning Miss Iowa, who of course wanted to be an actress, and I fear misguidedly felt that I might be some help in this direction. It's not always like that; on several other occasions I have departed New York with a collection of indifferent dismissals in various newspapers that I have been happy enough to leave on the plane.

In the eighties I effected an exchange programme between the Royal Court and Joseph Papp's Public Theater, and travelled to New York a great deal. Now on my 2012 visit, every morning Stella and I walked from Lafayette House, the boarding house where we were lodged, past the front door of The Public Theater to Culture Project on Lafayette and Bleecker. In the early eighties I had directed *Museum* by Tina Howe for The Public, and I recalled walking in those doors on the morning after the first preview. The African-American doorman grabbed me—'Hey Max,' he hollered, 'Joe came in five minutes ago and he liked the show! He told me!' I went up to the rehearsal room to give notes. All the actors were capering and dancing—'Joe likes the show,' they said, 'Joe likes the show.' He was a wonderful man, charismatic and extremely well read; some of the best conversations of my life came when I dropped into his office for a drink after rehearsals. It was a terrific kind of seminar/celebration.

Things on *Museum* hadn't started off so serenely. On the first day of rehearsals it emerged that the actors had been engaged on two different contracts. Those contracted early on had been promised $320 a week, but a new Equity waiver had been introduced whereby Off-Broadway theatres seating 299 or fewer need only pay $280. Actors contracted later were on this level. The rehearsal-room furniture had been structured carefully by the stage-management team; there was a semicircle of chairs for the sizeable (fourteen, I think) cast with one chair (for me) in the centre. Behind the semicircle was a discreet row of four chairs for the stage management themselves. I immediately sat with the actors in the semicircle so I could be part of the animated and agitated discussion about salary levels that ensued. The actors were unhappy. One of them rang the office, and before long Bernie Gersten, Joe's second-in-command, appeared to give details of the contractual situation and explain that

The Public was behaving perfectly legally. After he disappeared, the actors continued to fret, and rang the office again, demanding to speak to Joe himself. Eventually, word came back that he was on his way; immediate panic at their own boldness followed from the actors. One of the actors, Danny Hedaya, was appointed spokesman. Joe swept into the room and immediately took the single chair in the middle of the semicircle, which was now occupied for the first time. 'So you want to talk,' he challenged. Danny outlined the case that the actors had been contracted at different salary levels and that this was fundamentally unfair. Joe explained how hard up The Public was this particular year, but also offered a concession: 'Those of you who are family men, and women,' he said, 'I understand that things are particularly hard for you... we'll put you up to the higher level straight away, and, who knows, if the reviews are good and houses build up maybe we'll be in a position to put everybody up to the higher level.' The company tangibly relaxed; this was a substantial concession. However, Danny was not ready to relinquish his role as tribune, and launched into an eloquent speech. 'The Public had a great reputation for treating actors fairly,' he said. He had done a reading for the Public the year before for which he had been paid $25, which was great—he had been able to buy his girlfriend dinner at the Minetta Tavern. But now the actors were being asked to work as an ensemble and they should be paid an ensemble rate.

The actors were stunned into an embarrassed silence. Danny had way exceeded his brief. Joe had made a concession, and it had been rebuffed. They feared his response. After a silence that stretched for ever Joe spoke: 'Well, Danny, if what you're offering me is ensemble work at $320 a week I'd say I had a good deal.' Triumph. Cheers. The actors had won and Joe had conceded in the most graceful possible way. Joe walked round the semicircle shaking hands with the guys and kissing the girls on both cheeks. When he got to me at the end of the semicircle, he shook my hand like the others, but also put his other arm round my waist and pulled me towards him in what every-body construed as a gesture of fraternal friendship. But what he whispered in my ear was, 'This had better be a good show, English-man, or you're on the next fuckin' plane. Believe it.'

Joe was terrific. If I had learned about directing from Bill Gaskill, I learned about the joy and responsibility of heading a theatre from Joe Papp. We stayed friends and at some point in the mid-eighties he offered me a job. Well... for about twenty-five seconds. I had taken him to a matinee at the National Theatre, and I was driving Joe and his wife, Gail, to an evening play about boxing at the Half Moon. As we crossed Waterloo Bridge, Joe asked if I was interested in suc-ceeding him at The Public. 'It's about $100,000 a year,' he added, as if this vast sum was of peripheral interest. But by the time we reached the underpass at the end of the bridge he had retracted the offer. 'No, your work is here,' he said authoritatively, 'you must stay at the Royal Court for at least another five years.'

So April and early May 2012 found me back in a part of New York, the West Village, that was very familiar. Walking further afield one Sunday we also passed Andy Warhol's warehouse where I had once been to a party in the early seventies. This time I was in New York hanging out with the La MaMa company, who had made such an explosive impact at the Edinburgh Festival in 1968. I was really just a groupie, but I did operate a follow-spot in the first ever man-ifestation of *Hair*. Andy Warhol's party was quite lavish: the warehouse was the headquarters of his Playhouse of the Ridiculous Company. I did exchange a few words with Andy himself, but they were of such appropriate banality that I have forgotten them com-pletely. There was a buffet and I approached to get some food. A striking young woman was standing behind the trestle table. 'Hi,' she said, 'I'm Edie Sedgwick and I've got the wettest cunt in the whole of the Playhouse of the Ridiculous.' Startled by this bold statement I wasn't sure what protocol to follow, but I think I limply said, 'I'll just have some of the quiche, please.'

I enjoyed working on Chekhov's great play again, especially in Tom Kilroy's masterly adaptation. I had re-read David Thomson's extraordinary memoir *Woodbrook* to familiarise myself with the world of Anglo-Ireland, as well as having an instructive seminar with Professor Roy Foster, who reminded me that he had reviewed the original production of Kilroy's *Seagull* in 1981. *Woodbrook* is set in the late 1930s, so it is fifty years out of the correct period, but it tells the story of a young Englishman just down from Oxford who goes to Roscommon to act as tutor to the two daughters of a decaying Anglo-Irish family. In the course of the memoir he has clearly fallen in love with Ireland, but it's not clear till the end of the book that he reveals he has also tragically fallen in love with one of the two girls as well.

My notebook for *The Seagull* is full of background speculation about the characters. Are Pauline and Dr Hickey (Dorn) still having an affair in Act Four? (Probably not.) Does everybody believe Mary is Hickey's daughter? (Apparently Chekhov pointed to this more clearly in an earlier draft.) What happens to the characters when the play ends? (We imagined that under the Land Act, Gregory (Shamrayev) and Pauline were helped to buy fifteen acres of the Desmond (Arkadina) estate, and that Pauline introduced a new breed of French chickens to the West of Ireland—Roy Foster had told me that chickens were newly introduced on smallholdings following the Famine years—and that Pauline had a contract to deliver a basket of eggs twice weekly to the stationmaster at Ballinasloe Station, to be served in the dining cars of the Midland Great Western on the route to Dublin.) I had a doctor friend in New York who I had met when I was briefly and expensively hospitalised when directing J.T. Rogers' *The Overwhelming* in 2007. Under his supervision, we improvised Dr Hickey conducting a clinic in his surgery using only the medicines that would have been available to him in 1886. The other actors were patients. Back strain was endemic, but piles and prolapsed wombs featured too, and a nasty agricultural injury with a pitchfork led inevitably to an amputation in an age without antibiotics.

So: New York is always a heady and exciting town to work in, but I always return relieved that I don't have to actually earn a living there.

20th May 2012

Dear Frank,

Well I'm back! And the first thing to say is that my American adventure has made me much more affectionate to, and appreciative of, Arts Council England! I had forgotten how different it is to work for the unsubsidised American theatre, where all authority, decision-taking and financial decisions are in the hands of one key figure. The Culture Project is a small, relatively new but very ambitious not-for-profit organisation founded and run by Allan Buchman. It is smaller in scale but structurally identical to other not-for-profit organisations like The Public Theater or the Manhattan Theatre Club. The staff comprises one charismatic guy in charge and two dozen overambitious, overmotivated, overqualified, underpaid young women between 20 and 30 years of age who have excellent degrees from prestigious universities, and who have fancy titles like Development Director, Marketing Executive or Producing Director to disguise the fact that they have no real authority. For example, they can make a hotel booking, but they don't have the authority to use the credit card, so when you turn up, the booking has been cancelled because it has not been guaranteed. Similarly, Casting, Publicity and Sound Design are all outsourced, but by the time a prospective payment for these services has been authorised they have all taken other jobs. There appeared to be little or no difference between the Artistic Director's own bank account, and the funds pertaining to the organisation, so one was perpetually under an onerous personal obligation and at the same time concerned whether financial obligations could actually be met. There were to be two readings, one in the theatre itself (admission free but donation requested) and one in an upmarket apartment on Central Park West where admission was at $350 per ticket. In addition, rehearsals were open to the public, who paid $20 per rehearsal session. The actors were not paid but received minimal expenses.

We had three weeks' rehearsal and the Irish-American cast were extraordinarily committed and very talented. Perhaps because I'm accustomed to doing workshops in public, the open rehearsals were pleasant and worked well. The public were largely actors, directors, drama students, or ladies of a certain age whose children had left home, who were invariably enthusiastic and supportive. Over fifteen days of rehearsal there were over 300 admissions, and between $3,000 and $4,000 was raised from this source. The first performance was a truly magical evening; the actors were excellent, the public were appreciative and the occasion was blessed by the serendipitous presence of Alan Rickman, who had been in the 1981 production at the Royal Court.

The second performance was a bit of a car crash! The apartment where we played had fifty people crammed into a space which would comfortably have held only thirty. But above all, the apartment itself successfully upstaged the production; painted a shocking fuchsia pink, the flat of the eccentric millionairess owner was crammed full of artworks, some priceless, next to some straight from a junkshop; a Lowry, a Salvador Dalí above my head, a Polynesian statue at my elbow and a stuffed alligator crouching under a coffee table. I was sitting next to a doctor friend who leaned towards me as the performance started to say, 'Max, there's $5 million of plastic surgery in this room and I'm just talking above the neck.' It was hardly their fault that the apartment was unsuitable and that they couldn't see properly, but the audience were cantankerous and conservative. This was a brush with the dreaded New York subscription audience who so assiduously go to plays but aren't really playgoers. Every not-for-profit theatre in New York has a stodgy subscription audience that the poor actors have to wade through before they get to real people. Playwrights dread them and that is the reason why in 1985 Wally Shawn preferred to open *Aunt Dan and Lemon* at the Royal Court rather than in New York.

I was indeed offered a permanent job in New York with what can only be described as a shedload of money, but there was little temptation to accept it.

The real star of the venture was undoubtedly Tom Kilroy's adaptation, which after thirty years in hibernation emerged as fresh and sparkling as ever. It's very moving and funny.

Back at Out of Joint, the Friends scheme has received a magnificent donation from Danny Boyle, and I have also become a Friend myself by reverting part of my Culture Project fee to Out of Joint. This sum empowers me to nominate other Friends, so I would like to nominate you and George. No obligation is required on your part; you needn't even be friendly! But you would receive notice of all events and receive all the benefits accorded to Friends. This is an open offer made entirely without obligations on your part, but it occurs to me that you and George may feel compromised by being placed in such a position, however innocently the offer is made. I do hope not.

We have had an interesting and helpful meeting with a fundraiser, Emma Harris, who guided our first steps towards finding a sponsor. She thought the Gareth Thomas project would be appealing to sponsors, and we are just starting to cast the workshop week now in consultation with the National Theatre of Wales. A meeting with Sebastian Born [Literary Manager at the National Theatre] about the future of *This May Hurt A Bit* has been scheduled, and Tom Morris [Artistic Director of the Bristol Old Vic] will hold a reading in Bristol to coincide with the reopening of the Bristol Old Vic. Work on *Pitcairn* is scheduled for July with the RSC, and Tom Kilroy is confident of obtaining the Abbey's interest in a co-production of *The Seagull*. [It never happened. Fiach Mac Conghail is one of those people who infuriatingly never returns phone calls. It's easier to speak to the American Secretary of State than it is to the Artistic Director of the Abbey Theatre, Dublin.] Finally, plans for a short American tour of *A Dish of Tea with Dr Johnson* will be taken further this month; as a first step the Provost of Trinity College Dublin, my alma mater, has offered to host a performance in the salon of his beautiful Queen Anne house in the heart of Dublin. I am currently reading a new draft of *Scribblers* by Steve Waters, which is set in 1737 and which concerns the events that led up to the Licensing Act, by means of which Robert Walpole introduced censorship to the theatre. It's an important subject and were I running the Royal Court, who produce around eighteen plays a year, I would have no hesitation in programming it, but it has little obvious selling point and I fear it would fail to find a regional audience and could thus imperil our precious 'subsidy per seat' ratio. Thus are we pushed towards conservatism.

So Out of Joint feels very much alive and well, and it is very good to be back. I do hope you and George will feel able to accept the offer of Friendship! I look forward to hearing from you.

PS. In the financial year that has just ended, Out of Joint raised £4,696 from our newly launched Friends scheme. In the current financial year we have so far raised £8,616, already exceeding the target in the business plan of £4,000.

By this time Frank appeared to have grudgingly accepted that our experiences of diminishing attendances for new work in the regions was not unique. Shortly after my return from New York, Graham and I went to a further meeting at the Arts Council in Great Peter Street. It would be naively optimistic to claim that my bribe of Friendship had brought about any major change in the Arts Council's persona, but George Darling did say he accepted our concern that Out of Joint would be unable to continue developing and producing new work beyond the next three years at the current rate of funding. We would draw on our reserves (£425,000) in order to produce work over this three-year cycle, but this was not a course that could be pursued indefinitely. He reiterated how highly the Arts Council valued Out of Joint's work and how much they looked forward to continuing to fund us, but beyond these friendly words there was, of course, nothing tangible. It is clear that the diminished funding situation is fixed for the next three years, if not beyond. My correspondence with our Relationship Manager appeared to have achieved little except hopefully a slightly increased understanding on their part of the priorities and concerns that face us, notably the importance of research and development and the increased conservatism of regional audiences. The Arts Council had meanwhile insisted that Out of Joint should have a Clore Development Day, in which various arts administrators and financial experts would meet the Out of Joint board and management team to consider and comment on Out of Joint's business practices and on the help and support role played by the board. The Arts Council had become concerned, quite unreasonably I think, by the unchanging composition of Out of Joint's board and by the fact that so many of the board were themselves involved in the theatre one way or another. They had urged us to 'refresh' the board, and it was at this point that I recalled I had played rugby for Edinburgh Wanderers with Sir Menzies Campbell. He was an incredibly speedy wing, who scored several spectacular tries for Wanderers in the finals of the 1968 Middlesex Sevens. I recall labouring in his wake vainly hoping for a return pass that the increasing distance between us made impossible. I reached him through his office in the House of Commons. 'Is that Max Stafford-Clark, the plucky and talented scrum half?' he said. We arranged to have dinner at The Ivy. It was a hugely enjoyable evening, and he subsequently joined the Out of Joint board as an observer. I reported on these events to Frank Endwright on 28th May:

Dear Frank,

I am delighted that you and George have become Friends. Over the last month, both here and in New York, I have spent some time pursuing new board members in an attempt to refresh the board. I have met with limited success. When I finally got through to Hillary Clinton she laughed at the suggestion. I guess she has her hands full saving the free world at the moment. Anna Ford said she had spent too much time already 'on charitable projects' and she wanted to direct this part of her life to herself. Sir Menzies Campbell, however, was enthusiastic and is coming to the next board meeting (18th June) as an observer. I hadn't realised he had been chair of the board of the Edinburgh Lyceum for three years. He will be a great addition.

The Clore Day was both informative and entertaining. Obviously we await their report, but they appeared very positive about the role of the board. Some time was spent in examining how we could ensure that the Arts Council would look favourably on Out of Joint in the next round of funding awards in 2015. Opinion was split as to whether Out of Joint's cause would be better served by a huge success (thus proving we were indispensable to ACE's plans) or a huge flop (thus proving how needy we were). However, this is one event which will perforce take care of itself! Their advice about the accumulation of reserves was cautionary. On the one hand they were impressed that they will help see us through the next three years, but on the other hand their advice was that it was a double-edged sword to place in the Arts Council's hands and that undoubtedly the over-impressive reserves had played a part in your assessment of our needs in the last round of funding awards.

I have had a meeting with an American tour booker who is keen to take *A Dish of Tea with Dr Johnson* on an American tour in March 2013. The situation is made slightly more complicated by the presence of Ian Redford in both *Our Country's Good* and *A Dish of Tea with Dr Johnson*. If *Our Country's Good* were to transfer after its initial run at the St James Theatre it would become necessary to recast his role. However, this is a problem we should be so lucky to have! [*Our Country's Good* was to play a six-week season at the new St James Theatre from 28th January following its autumn tour.]

Cambridge have pulled out of the final tour week of *Our Country's Good* as they wish to start their Christmas show earlier. Decisions about ticket pricing for the St James run of *Our Country's Good* have been taken. The price for student access and schools groups is £15. Personally I feel this is too high: clearly lowering the price would adversely affect our finances, but I believe it would make the play more accessible and thus increase the audience. I have sent *Scribblers* by Steve Waters to both Ian Rickson and to Jessica Swale: both are directors who have expressed enthusiasm at working for Out of Joint.

Casting for both *Our Country's Good* and the Gareth Thomas project continues, the latter in conjunction with the National Theatre of Wales.

Even in retrospect it still seems outrageous that the Arts Council were able to push through such cuts without censure of any kind or condemnation from the press. I didn't feel it was the Fourth Estate's finest moment. Perhaps this is unsurprising in a political climate when all the major parties were trumpeting their enthusiasm for austerity. But Liz Forgan's [chair of the Arts Council] claim that the cuts were made on the basis of clear and logical criteria seems not just economical with the truth, but an outrageous misrepresentation. I'm no economist, but it seemed to me that the headlong rush to austerity had also gone unexamined. After all, the Napoleonic Wars finished in 1815, but it was 1959 before the debt they incurred was paid off. My advice to George Osborne would be borrow, borrow, borrow. Heed not the consequences; my daughter, Kitty, and her children can look after themselves!

6th June 2012

Dear Frank,

Well, I lost the argument about student prices for *Our Country's Good*. It remains at £15. Graham is convinced that the break even would be unattainable if we went for a lower price. Following our experience in New York with *The Seagull* we have agreed to 'open' rehearsals of *Our Country's Good* to the public. It will be limited to twelve people in any one session and there will be three open sessions of one-and-a-half hours per day. We will charge £6 to each person (students £5) or £12 (£10) for a three-session all-day ticket.

I have been in correspondence with Joanna Reid, Principal of LAMDA, and she has agreed that I can use next year's 'Long Project' with second-year students to develop a new version of *Love and a Bottle*, George Farquhar's first play, which I have written to you about earlier. This will involve working with the students from May to July next year twice a week, in which time I hope to develop through improvisation some alternative storylines for Farquhar's characters and workshop a new version of the play.

I sent Jim Broadbent *Scribblers* by Steve Waters and he has
responded very positively. It may be that I have
underestimated the play. I am reading a biography of Joe
Papp at the moment, and he writes: 'I continually plead a
certain ignorance over things that are new. It's very hard to
adjust to a new artist.' Certainly, when I was attending Royal
Court script meetings I missed the visceral innovation of
Blasted by Sarah Kane, and it would have been a play I would
have passed on. I have been warned!

Things were indeed healthy at Out of Joint, but as is so often the case
in the new-writing theatre, a lot of our new work existed only in my
head and was not yet present on the page! *This May Hurt A Bit* was
the exception. Stella was finalising the draft we would read in Bristol at the end of June, but I had obtained only three days of
preparation for a reading of Richard Bean's *Pitcairn,* while a delivery
draft of Rebecca Lenkiewicz's *Witches,* and my version of George Farquhar's *Love and a Bottle,* were still in the future. As was Robin Soans's
new verbatim project, based on Bridgend and the life of Gareth
Thomas, which was the project I was to embark on next.

18th June 2012

Dear Frank,

I returned on Saturday from Bridgend in South Wales, where I
have been conducting a development workshop for a week
with seven actors and a writer. There are two particular stories
we have been pursuing: one is that of the iconic Welsh rugby
star, Gareth Thomas, who won 105 caps for Wales, captained
both Wales and the British and Irish Lions and 'came out' as
gay in December 2009. The other strand is the tragic epidemic
of teenage suicides that took place in 2006/7 and which
involved over thirty young people in Bridgend. Bridgend
College provided rehearsal space and many of the young
people we interviewed were currently attending the college.
Gareth Thomas was massively impressive, and the simplicity

and dignity with which he told his story affected us all, as did the stories of the students we talked to, many of whom come from broken and dysfunctional families and who had found a support and a structure to their lives from the college itself. It was an inspiring week, and our partner, the National Theatre of Wales, helped cast a talented and formidable team of young actors. As my earlier correspondence has emphasised, research and development has been and continues to be a crucial element of Out of Joint's work, and one for which we have been extremely successful at securing creative partners and financial support.

The next step for *Wearing the Raven*, which is the provisional title for the Welsh project, is to commission Robin Soans, who promises a delivery by Christmas. The National Theatre of Wales are almost fully programmed for 2013 so a production date in early 2014 looks most likely. Tom Morris at the Bristol Old Vic is eager to do a reading of *This May Hurt A Bit* on 26th July, as part of the launch of his new season. It will be terrific for Stella to hear the play, but I am putting more faith in the development week at the National Theatre Studio which has now been confirmed for the week of 22nd October. I am about to start casting *Pitcairn* (by Richard Bean) with the RSC's casting team as that reading takes place on 25th July after three days' work.

Following the open rehearsals for *The Seagull* in New York, I decided to go ahead and emulate that scheme with *Our Country's Good*. A small piece appeared in the *Evening Standard* and within two days we have sold all the available tickets (it is limited to six people per session). Over 120 people have booked and the money raised is just over £1,000 in two days [a bit optimistic – it was £825]. I am thrilled although slightly alarmed; since we are still casting I haven't been able to tell the actors, so I hope I haven't made a rod for my own back. I don't want to be forced to continue this experiment for every rehearsal by an economic imperative. It should be seen as an imaginative and temporary ploy to increase our income that may or may not be desirable in the long run, but we have certainly discovered an appetite and a market!

Gareth Thomas had led the warm-up every morning in the college. It culminated in a game of British Bulldog, where one actor had had to pick up Gareth and move him backward ten yards. We also re-enacted some of Gareth's most famous tries. Wee Bethan Witcomb, one of the actresses in the workshop company, played Ian Gough catching the ball in the line-out. She looked like a salmon leaping from the water as she was hoisted by the boys to secure the ball for Wales. We went through various titles for the play—*Wearing the Raven* was the first. Apparently, the raven was the Bridgend team's emblem, and as a boy Gareth had wanted nothing more than to 'wear the raven'. This was succeeded by *The Other Reason*, a phrase that the ex-Wales coach Scott Johnson had suggested was the cause of Gareth's manifest unhappiness. But eventually we settled on *Crouch, Touch, Hold, Engage*, which is the mantra the referee chants to set the scrum. Or at least it was. He now says 'crouch, touch, set', but that doesn't sound so interesting—and the scrum in professional rugby isn't what it was, either. It just collapses every time these days, so perhaps our advocacy of past habits might encourage a return to former stability in the scrum as well!

During this period I had also been reading and re-reading *Scribblers* by Steve Waters. This tells of the young Henry Fielding's random encounter with Robert Walpole, the first Prime Minister, and their increasingly bitter relationship as Fielding is duped into writing a play so manifestly offensive that Walpole is enabled to introduce the Licensing Act, which imposed censorship on the English stage for over two hundred years.

2nd July 2012

Dear Frank,

Thank you for seeing me and Graham the week before last. I'm not sure if I expressed my concerns about developing work for next year forcefully enough. In the long term I am very confident about a number of the projects we have in hand: *This*

May Hurt A Bit, *Love and a Bottle*, *Pitcairn*, *Wearing the Raven* (the Gareth Thomas project) and *Witches*. However, I am less certain that any of them will be ready to go into rehearsal in 2013. I have read *Scribblers* by Steve Waters again and although there are wonderful things in it, it tells the story more from Walpole's point of view than Fielding's. With ten people, *The Seagull* is too expensive to contemplate, despite co-production interest from America. I had an interview with somebody from the Victoria and Albert Museum last week, who are publishing a book entitled *Played in Britain: Modern Theatre in 100 Plays*. I was astonished but gratified to learn that *The Arbor* by Andrea Dunbar was on her list. Perusing the list of one hundred plays, there were several I would have questioned, but Andrea's work has certainly grown in stature since the early eighties and remains a compelling document of that time. So I guess that's a contender too.

I spent the beginning of last week at the National Student Drama Festival in Sheffield, where I gave two workshops. At £75 a time it was hardly cost-effective with train fares and two nights in a hotel, but I hope it is effective missionary work; a party of students from Aberystwyth promptly booked for the visit of *Our Country's Good* in October.

I have also had several meetings with bookers and producers from America in an attempt to pin down the tour of *A Dish of Tea with Dr Johnson*, which remains elusive. 'Why don't you do *Hedda Gabler*?' said one booking agent. 'I could sell that.' It was ever thus. It seems Samuel Johnson is 'threatening' in the United States: they would prefer Charles Dickens. I guess we were two years too early with *Andersen's English*, Sebastian Barry's play about Hans Christian Andersen's stay with the Dickens family.

9th July 2012

Dear Frank,

It's been a hard week; dominated by several long planning meetings both with Karl Sydow, the co-producer of *Our Country's Good* at the St James Theatre, and Allan Buchman from Culture Project in New York. Allan is very keen that we should turn *The Seagull* into a full production in New York. In the first instance Graham and I had approached the notion as a co-production using the American actors as the basis of a company over here, but on further exploration, bringing American actors to England was discovered to be prohibitively expensive, not simply in terms of fares and per diems, but the other myriad demands made by American Equity. Allan then undertook to produce it simply as an American project in New York. At first I said I could see no window for that until late 2013/early 2014, mindful that Out of Joint was committed to two productions next year. Graham and I were also keen to revive the much more manageable *A Dish of Tea with Dr Johnson* both in New York, where it could possibly make a profit, and to tour for a couple more weeks in the UK, where it would boost our number of touring weeks in the current financial year. In the end we proposed a compromise plan that will involve rehearsing *The Seagull* while *Dr Johnson* is playing in New York. This will enable me to return in time to pick up the development period for *Love and a Bottle* we have been offered by LAMDA.

I enclose a copy of a letter to me from Ian Redford. Ian has been an almost permanent member of Out of Joint's company for the last ten years, having done at least a dozen productions. He wants to miss a week of rehearsals for *Our Country's Good* to do a lucrative film in South Africa. I had conditionally agreed to this; the condition being that he and his agent should join Out of Joint's Friends scheme. He had agreed, but my reminder to him was seen as provocative, and he replied with some irritation. All is peaceable now, but I enclose the letter to emphasise what pressure we are under to improve the wages of senior actors if we are to retain their loyalty and the standard of acting.

Hopefully the schedule for *Dr Johnson* and *The Seagull* will be resolved in the coming week. The money raised in the current year from the Friends scheme is £14,002, and the number of Friends is now 46.

Ian's letter read:

Dear Max,

Thanks for the card. We had already talked about the Friends scheme when you agreed for me to go to South Africa to do this small part in the film. I told you the amount to reiterate that it was necessary for me to take part in the *Our Country's Good* project. So I can only imagine that you think I am getting a small fortune for the job and some of that should go to redress the balance from Out of Joint's cut in grant.

It's not the first time we have come up against this. Actors work for Out of Joint not because they have to but because they want to, because they believe in your method of working, the quality of the scripts, the opportunity to practise what they originally entered the profession for, and quite simply because there isn't anybody out there who can match you.

However, it does mean a cut in wages, and quite often a loss, inasmuch as the performers are also subsidising Out of Joint. The rising cost of living, especially in London, means that actors more often than not are losing money which they hope to make up in other areas of the business – TV, radio, voice-overs, and, very rarely, film.

I recently was offered a year's contract in the West End which I turned down out of loyalty to you, which would have made a profit of £48,000.

I was sorry to have irritated Ian, who has grown in stature enormously as an actor over the years I have been working with him, and who has given Out of Joint exemplary service. His Dr Johnson, Mr Hardcastle (*She Stoops to Conquer*) and his Harry Brewer (*Our Country's Good*) were all excellent leading performances. I made my peace and all was well between us.

It was gratifying to find the funds from the Friends scheme rising so consistently, but the scheme needed constant prompting and attention. I was becoming a full-time fundraiser and a part-time director, but this was seemingly the direction in which we were being pushed. My experience of Culture Project should have alerted me. Looking back at my reports to Frank Endwright on the slowness of negotiations in New York, I feel I should have realised earlier than I did that an eventual production was unlikely.

23rd July 2012

Dear Frank,

I have been in Ireland briefly making plans for the performance of *A Dish of Tea with Dr Johnson* in the salon of the Provost's House in Trinity College. The plan is that after two weeks of English touring, we will do a single performance in Dublin on 25th March before flying to New York. The room in the Provost's house is exquisite. The house was built in 1780 so the period is perfect: the Provost will host a reception following the performance. The only drawback is that it is a private house and college statutes prevent us from charging for the performance. We will approach the British Council but I am hopeful Graham will be able to find one or two one-night stands in England on the Monday and Tuesday of that week to soften the blow. Meanwhile, negotiations with the Culture Project proceed at an agonisingly slow pace. There is no doubt that they really really want to produce *The Seagull*, and will put up with *A Dish of Tea with Dr Johnson* for three weeks in order to get it. But their enthusiasm is more than amply balanced and checked by their inefficiency, so arrangements are slow to take a final shape.

I had a very good meeting with Steve Waters last week (author of *Scribblers*). He promises a new version by September. What is a 'good' meeting? Well, I suppose it's one in which I am able to articulate my reservations and suggestions with clarity and precision and where the writer embraces these with enthusiasm, or at least pretends to. A good meeting doesn't always lead to a good play, but a bad meeting never does. The meeting with Steve was very good, whereas my final meeting with Frank McGuinness (*Love and a Bottle*) was as bad as they get! So the autumn 2013 show is looking more and more like a choice between *Scribblers* and a revival of *The Arbor*. I am reluctant to programme yet another revival from the eighties – after *Top Girls, Our Country's Good* and *The Seagull* this would be the fourth from this period and the third for Out of Joint. But, extraordinary to relate, this first play by a fifteen-year-old Bradford schoolgirl has excited much academic comment in the intervening thirty years. Both Professor Elaine Aston (University of Lancaster) and Professor Janelle Reinelt (University of Warwick) have written extensively on Andrea's work. She would have been astonished. Do the Arts Council have a view about programming a third revival?

I conclude with another quote from my reading of Joe Papp's biography. He said, 'Once in every ten years or so a play comes along that fulfils my original idea of what role theatre must play in society.' *The Arbor* comes near to being that sort of play. At the same time my search for 'non-threatening' work continues. I even read *The Pirates of Penzance* last week hoping I could turn the Major General into a UN officer, the pirates into Somali pirates and the Major General's daughter into a party of schoolgirls taken hostage, but in the end the plot is just too silly!

Frank came to the reading of *Pitcairn* in the Out of Joint rehearsal room in July. The play powerfully and shockingly depicts the disintegration of the little community on Pitcairn established by Fletcher Christian as the natives murdered the whites and then the native women murdered the native men. When the Royal Navy stumbled across Pitcairn seventeen years later (it had been incorrectly charted), there was one mutineer who had survived, together with a number of children and native women. It is an extraordinary and largely untold story of utopia turning into chaos and horror. One of the particular problems is that the play demands three Polynesian actors and eight Polynesian actresses. Comb Spotlight as much as you like, but that's a challenge. Do we then assume that any ethnic exotica, Asian, African-Caribbean or Tahitian will do, or do we go for 'colour-blind' casting where everybody can be Polynesian? I opted for the latter, thus introducing the gene of red hair to Polynesia for the first time. I think Richard's rendition of the story is pellucid and clear, but even were we to take the politically incorrect but historically accurate step of having topless Tahitian maidens, it's not an upbeat story. At one moment, Christian reflects sadly, 'I now think less of humanity than I once did. I know now that the natural condition of man is violence, lechery, drunkenness, greed, suspicion and hatred for his fellow man.' Nick Hytner had, I think, found the play repugnant and rejected it straight away, but I think it is terrific. Frank Endwright liked it too:

25th July 2012

Dear Max,

Good to see you on Weds. I thought it worth reiterating how much I liked the play and how I thought it worked so well on so many levels. I agree with you that the play would be enriched if the political-historical context could be brought out of the writing a bit more – not that that is a weakness that needs addressing, but it just feels that there is more and more depth and colour that could be added… I also thought that it's unusual to see a large-cast play where all of the characters have interesting journeys as opposed to the 4 or 5 'main' characters. Please let me know how it progresses.

I can see that *The Arbor* is a great play and worthwhile reviving. My concern – and this is obviously one you share – is the timing of it after three other revivals; I'm not sure how this might be perceived by venues, audiences, critics (irrespective of the quality of the piece itself). I guess the programming of it would carry a risk of affecting the perception of where Out of Joint were headed. I don't know how great that risk is or how significant that changed perception would be. But I think it needs thinking about and discussing.

From an Arts Council perspective, yes, we primarily fund you to produce new work and accept the occasional revival where there is good reason. I think I'd like to hear a bit more about your considerations of what the potential downsides might be, if they matter and, if so, what (if anything) might be done – and also a bit more about the other options available. After that, I think we'd find it easier to arrive at a view.

Hope Stella's reading went well.

Well done again for *Pitcairn*.

The mutiny on the *Bounty* occurred in the same year (1789) as the French Revolution, eight years before the naval mutinies at Spithead and on the Nore, and two years before the formation of the United Irish Movement by Wolfe Tone. The principal lesson I learned from the reading was that the play needed to be contextualised. It took place at a time when revolution was in the air. Tom Paine's *The Rights of Man* was a bestseller, and certainly the ideas therein would have been familiar to the officers on the *Bounty*. Unless the extraordinary events in the play are presented as a gesture towards utopia and justifiable revolution, the play would become a serial and sickening catalogue of brutal murders. Perhaps this is what Nick Hytner feared when he resolved that the National Theatre would not co-produce it with us.

I should explain that although I did history at A level and indeed read Irish History as a subsidiary subject at Trinity, I am not a historian. The past for me is a Sahara of ignorance spotted with the occasional oasis or puddle of knowledge and reading grouped round the date of a particular play. For example, 1706 (*The Recruiting Officer*), 1788 (*Our Country's Good*), 1737 (the Licensing Act and *Scribblers*), 1620 (*A Jovial Crew*) or 1886 (Kilroy's Irish *Seagull*) would all be contenders for my specialist subject on *Mastermind*. There aren't many plays from the late eighteenth century still in the repertoire. There is Sheridan, of course, and it's little short of a theatrical disaster that politics rather than theatre was the obsession of the second half of his life. I had directed *She Stoops to Conquer* (1773), but sadly Goldsmith did not live long after writing his masterpiece and died at thirty-three, and I hadn't read widely round the period. Nonetheless, even the most cursory acquaintance with the late eighteenth century leads to the question: why did England not emulate France and America? Why was there no revolution in this country? The mutiny on the *Bounty* and its aftermath is a microcosm of the yearning for utopia, and the sometimes murderous consequences that follow that.

30th July 2012

Dear Frank,

What a week for Out of Joint! I think we're on the trail of two enormously exciting plays. Both need further work but both have huge potential. After *Pitcairn*, Stella and I went down to Bristol where Tom Morris had assembled an appropriately stellar cast to read Stella's play *This May Hurt A Bit*. The cast included Miranda Richardson, Stephanie Cole, Toby Jones, Oliver Cotton, Richard Johnson and Danny Sapani. It was a terrific evening and even with just one day's rehearsal the end is unbearably moving and powerful. It was extraordinarily serendipitous to witness Danny Boyle's tribute to the NHS in the Olympic opening ceremony 24 hours later! But the most important thing is that Stella is full of ideas for how to develop the play further.

Thank you so much both for coming to *Pitcairn* and for responding to my question about programming *The Arbor*. As you know, I share your concerns, although I am not too worried about public or critical perception. We will of course blame the Arts Council! I realise this is hardly fair since it's more lack of time rather than lack of resources that puts us in this dilemma. But, hey, who cares about fairness? Certainly not Arts Council England. But an alternative is on the horizon. A few weeks ago I met Dawn King, author of *Foxfinder*, which was hailed by Michael Billington as one of the most powerful new plays of 2011. I regularly hold meetings with interesting writers and in the course of our conversation Dawn said she had delivered the first draft of a commission for the West Yorkshire Playhouse. We were discussing a fresh commission but I asked to read this so I could familiarise myself with her work. She sent me *Ciphers*, a play about a young woman who is recruited by MI5 and the deadly impact this has on her private life. I found it very powerful, but when I rang to congratulate her she told me the new regime at the West Yorkshire Playhouse had passed on the play and that it was available.

So here are the runners and riders for the Out of Joint 2013 Autumn Stakes with appropriate odds crudely attached for the likelihood of rehearsal a year from now in August 2013:

1. CIPHERS by Dawn King. With a cast of four, an acclaimed new writer and a couple of vivid sex scenes, this late entrant becomes a favourite. Blanche McIntyre, who has worked at Out of Joint as an Associate Director and who directed *Foxfinder* very successfully, could direct, which would give her a chance and me a break. A relatively unknown writer, so it comes into the 'threatening' category despite its other advantages. 5/1 favourite.

2. SCRIBBLERS by Steve Waters. Cast of at least nine so more expensive. Deals with Walpole's introduction of the Licensing Act and the subsequent two hundred years of state censorship, and traces Henry Fielding's journey from playwright to novelist. I await a new draft due in September. An important subject but not obviously audience-friendly. The new draft would have to be a considerable improvement. 12/1.

3. THE ARBOR by Andrea Dunbar. Would be the third (not fourth, *The Seagull* was not an Out of Joint production) consecutive Out of Joint revival from the eighties and we have rehearsed the reasons why this would not be desirable. But academic interest and the thought of editing a new version from the existing material still makes it attractive. 8/1.

4. PITCAIRN by Richard Bean. Richard already has plans to reduce the cast size from eighteen to sixteen, but it would still be an impossibility for Out of Joint to produce singlehanded. Greg Doran and the RSC were enthusiastic but have yet to declare a commitment. In any case the RSC have no available slot for new writing until late 2013/early 2014. 25/1.

5. THIS MAY HURT A BIT by Stella Feehily. One family's journey through the digestive system of the NHS. Clearly a very important and very Out of Joint subject. Further development at the National Theatre Studio in October, but even if Nick Hytner and the RNT were interested, the Cottesloe is closed for 2013. 25/1.

6. WITCHES by Rebecca Lenkiewicz. Following the workshop in February, Rebecca is due to deliver a first draft at Christmas. 30/1.

7. GARETH THOMAS by Robin Soans (aka *Crouch, Touch, Hold, Engage*). Currently going through contractual wrangling with Gareth's agent, but following workshop last June, Robin is also due to deliver by Christmas. 30/1.

8. LOVE AND A BOTTLE by George Farquhar, adapted by Stella Feehily. Development work scheduled with LAMDA students from May 2013. 50/1.

9. Roy Williams. Commissioned six years ago. In the intervening time Roy has shown us two plays which were in fact rejected commissions by the Tricycle and the RSC respectively. He has promised a delivery by Christmas. I have my doubts. 50/1.

10. Nina Raine. Another long-term commission. (Five years?) She has written two scenes and is writing about a lawyer having an affair with an actress. She will deliver eventually, but when? 66/1.

11. Timberlake Wertenbaker. A new commission for which we unsuccessfully petitioned you for funds before Christmas. She is writing about the Basque Revolutionary Movement (ETA). 100/1.

12. You never know what else may turn up. 150/1.

From this rather flippant précis you will see that in the medium term there is much strong work about which I am very confident. The options for the short term (to rehearse a year from now) are fewer. I hope this emphasises the continued and continual importance of development work to Out of Joint.

Negotiations with Culture Project about *Dr Johnson* and *The Seagull* grind on. We are nearer fixing dates for the programme although this has involved dropping one of the English touring weeks. This is to avoid playing in New York in the week of 27th May when there are a number of public holidays. Our number of English touring weeks in 2012/13 would thus be eleven, with one in Wales, one in Dublin, one in Holland and three in the United States. It is a rich mix but it will equal the lowest number of English touring weeks in any year of Out of Joint's history. This is a sad but inevitable consequence of the reduced funding and of restricting our output to a single production. We would like to do more! You know it makes sense…

It was time once more to cease speculation about the future and focus on the present. On Monday 30th July 2012, I started rehearsals for Timberlake Wertenbaker's play *Our Country's Good*. This was at least the fourth or fifth occasion on which I had directed the play; originally in 1988, revived for Australia in 1989, in Los Angeles in 1991 and again at the Young Vic and on tour in 1998. In post-show discussions during this new production I was to be asked regularly what the differences were between previous productions and the one I essayed this time round. I found it very difficult to answer: of course, the personalities of the actors were different, and certainly academic studies of Aboriginal life had moved on since 1988, but I had no new concept with which to approach Timberlake's play. I wondered whether this would be the case for everyone who came to see it. Would fond memories of the productions in 1988 or 1998 be used as a cudgel to beat the production with by audience or critics? In the event this didn't happen, but it was certainly a concern.

Perhaps most pertinently, and with bitter irony, history was repeating itself as we went back into rehearsal. The theatre had been under threat in 1988, but I believe Cameron and Osborne have inflicted more damage on theatre infrastructure, and eroded the morale of the theatre community far more effectively in three years than Mrs Thatcher managed in three terms.

When casting, I always endeavour to carry some kind of semi-permanent company in my head. On this occasion I had worked with one actor (Ian Redford) many times, with two others on two or three productions (Lisa Kerr and Kathryn O'Reilly), and with two other actors on one previous occasion (Helen Bradbury and Ciaran Owens). So there were five members of the company who were familiar with the working methods I used, and five for whom it would be a new experience. This was an excellent situation, and as near as one can get to a permanent company in England.

6th August 2012

Dear Frank,

I started rehearsals for *Our Country's Good* last week and as far as I can tell it's going extremely well; certainly the actors have absorbed our six paying guests without any trouble. [I was wrong.] William Gaskill came in and took one session of rehearsal much to my delight. I have been trying to get him involved with Out of Joint's work since before *Macbeth* in 2004. At one point he agreed to direct *All That Fall* by Samuel Beckett, but the rights proved impossible to obtain. Now he has concluded work at RADA, Bill has been virtually retired, yet he remains one of the most radical and charismatic of European directors. It can never be at the centre of Out of Joint's mission, but to sustain the careers of senior directors as well as giving opportunities to younger directors is something I am delighted to do. Des Kennedy, who was Out of Joint's Associate Director for six months last year and for whom we received special funding from ACE remains as Associate Director on *Our Country's Good*, and is now able to take additional responsibilities both in rehearsal and with the education workshops. To date in the last nineteen years I have directed 35 of Out of Joint's 37 productions, but it would be good for both me and for the company to have the occasional dialogue with another director. I hope that in future we can once again obtain special funding from you for this purpose.

We continue to negotiate with Culture Project in New York, but now the dates for *Dr Johnson* and *The Seagull* have been more or less fixed, we have to address the difficult issue of American Equity as there are three English or Irish actors in the cast. Design is also tricky. Clearly it's easier and cheaper for Culture Project to employ an American designer, but I know from experience that design consultations over the phone are extremely inaccurate and unsatisfactory, and I have no plans or time to be in New York before the end of March.

I will write again with further developments. You are most welcome to rehearsals of *Our Country's Good* at any time. We rehearse in London till 18th August.

Equity is a powerful force in New York, and their initial ruling was that not only should the three non-American actors be paid at a rate of $970 per week instead of the proposed $425, but that the whole company should be lifted to this eye-watering rate of pay. The lesson seemed to be, 'If you want non-American actors, you have to pay for it!'

I was indeed thrilled to get Bill Gaskill back into the rehearsal room. We had last worked together nearly forty years previously, when we co-directed the first three productions for Joint Stock—*The Speakers, Fanshen* and *Yesterday's News*. His influences had been from Brecht and the Berliner Ensemble, whereas mine had been from the La MaMa company and some of the wilder European experimental companies. He was very much the senior partner and from him I had learned both precision and the importance of a political analysis. I think what I gave him was the confidence to leave the proscenium and embark on the 'promenade' staging that featured in *The Speakers*. I'm not sure how much we really had in common, but we both persuaded ourselves that we did, and certainly good work came of it. In the intervening years we had stayed friends, and he was very kind to me when I was in hospital. He would regularly come to see my productions at the Royal Court, but would also regularly make his departure in the interval, saying, 'I had seen the actors and I could tell what the end would be, so there didn't seem any point in staying.' This puzzled the front-of-house staff, who said, 'I thought he was supposed to be your friend.' But it didn't puzzle me; I expected no less from his acute and pitiless judgement. Nor were things perfectly harmonious on *Our Country's Good*. On the first morning he took rehearsal, we had agreed on two scenes he would work on. I thought I would arrive about midday to see how he was getting on. As I limped down the alleyway to Out of Joint, Stella and I met a fleeing Helen Bradbury, our excellent Dabby Bryant. She was in fact going to get a coffee from the Atlas Café, but she said, 'I'm running away, he's pasting us round the walls.' She was joking, but after the break I began to see what she meant. In two-and-a-half hours Bill had barely advanced three pages. He constantly confronted the actors' decisions and ruthlessly exposed their shortcomings. To those that could surmount the challenge there was much to learn, particularly in terms of phrasing, punctuation and character. But it was hard. 'Is that any better, Bill?' pleaded a desperate John Hollingworth, who knew Bill well because he had worked with him at RADA. 'No, no, no. Not in the slightest,' responded Bill immediately. I began to understand that forty years earlier in Joint Stock we had probably played Good Cop, Bad Cop, or at least Soft Cop, Hard Cop. He had not mellowed over the years.

Perhaps Bill was intrigued by how 'other' the Traverse Workshop Company seemed. In the early 1970s we had been invited to the Come Together Festival which he had promoted at the Royal Court. This was a deliberate attempt on Bill's part to involve the Royal Court in the work of disparate British fringe companies. We had been unable to attend as we had already accepted an invitation to an International Theatre Institute Conference outside Paris. This turned out to be an unforgettable event.

There were Italian, French, Polish, American, Swiss and Swedish companies, as well as the Traverse Workshop Company representing Scotland. The event took place in an upmarket holiday camp in the leafy fringes of Paris. The weather was gorgeous and the first day was spent in a fractious and irritable discussion about what we were going to do for a week. We resolved to stage some part of our work for each other. The Swiss group then spontaneously and impressively launched into a surreal improvisation in the middle of the discussion. The Marxist French group appeared at dinner mummified in bandages from head to foot. They sat wordlessly at different tables in protest at the bourgeois decadence of the whole conference. It proved rather a conversation killer. The Americans were represented by Robert Wilson who had made an installation outside the rehearsal room. It featured a skinned rabbit and it was a good thing that the conference only lasted a week, as by Friday it had begun to pong a bit. I forget about the Italian group's performance, but they certainly gave the best parties at which they grew drunk and tearful with rigorous application. They were largely shop assistants from Turin who had persuaded their mothers that they were going to a high-level academic conference. Their director was a fierce and autocratic maestro who at the initial conference had announced unforgettably, '*Dans ma compagnie c'est mois je suis le chef.*' The Polish group were Tadeusz Kantor, the famous troupe from Kraków, who gave a dignity to the entire conference. We posed as a Scottish Liberation group which was entirely false but at least earned a modicum of respect from the French Marxists. However, the most impressive group was undoubtedly the Swedes, who had commandeered the title National Theatre of Sweden. They announced that their performance would be al fresco outside their chalet. We arrived late and clearly the performance had already started. About 250 people, hushed and attentive, were sitting on the ground overlooking the grassy bowl in front of the Swedish chalet. As we came closer we could see a very beautiful young man with blond hair down to his waist slowly and purposefully fucking the very beautiful leading lady on the rug in the centre of the arena. She writhed sensuously between his attentions as the audience craned forward to get a better view. I don't know what this had to do with theatre, but Bill was mightily impressed with the story.

6th August 2012

Dear Max,

Thank you for your email and for your equine-themed letter. The *Ciphers*-horse sounds both intriguing and exciting. From what you wrote, it sounds like the script doesn't need much (any?) development work on it. I look forward to hearing more about it.

Quite randomly, at the behest of my three-year-old (!) at the weekend I watched a David Attenborough documentary (on YouTube) called *The Lost Gods of Easter Island*. It had quite a bit about the early contact between Europeans and the inhabitants of Easter Island and Polynesia in the late eighteenth century. It of course reminded me of *Pitcairn*. If you've got a spare 45 minutes, it may be worth a look – in any case, it's quite interesting in its own right.

How amazing that William Gaskill took a rehearsal session for *Our Country's Good*. I would imagine (hope?) that the actors were both awe-struck and inspired. Thank you for your invitation to attend a rehearsal, which I would be delighted to take up. I think I could do either Tues or Thurs morning next week – would either of these work for you? If so, I should be able to confirm before the end of the week.

Hopefully see you soon.

13th August 2012

Dear Frank,

Rehearsals continue for *Our Country's Good*. At this point the agony for a director is whether to press forward with alacrity and get in a good number of runthroughs or to go slower,

accumulate detail and leave lots of runthroughs to previews. I
tend to favour the second, but on this occasion it is rather
forced on me because Ian Redford is in South Africa for a week
filming and Laura Dos Santos is in Ireland tomorrow
(grandmother's funeral). The actors have absorbed our paying
guests although they admit that they have been occasionally
inhibited by their presence. For example, Mary Brenham's
shame at losing her virginity or the death of Duckling Smith's
lover are both incidents where in more private circumstances I
might have asked for the actors' own emotional recall of similar
experiences. To date we have received £475 in matured
admissions to rehearsal, and I have also taken the opportunity
of their presence to sell them £190 worth of books. Not all of
the latter is profit as I haven't deducted the cost of the books
to Out of Joint, but both represent a healthy increase in income
streams. The response of the attendees has been universally
ecstatic, albeit their ecstasy has been expressed in rather more
restrained terms than the Americans who came to rehearsals of
The Seagull, who were wont to say 'awesome', 'magical', 'life-
changing' and similar overexuberant expressions of approval.
The lesson for me is that I must stop thinking of the paying
audience as simply a cynical manoeuvre to increase our
income streams at your behest – and embrace it as a valid
educational experiment that is properly a part of Out of Joint's
mission. The advance looks good. 40% tickets already sold in
Bolton: 3,273 tickets sold and that doesn't include
reservations. Bookings are promising everywhere else too,
except Aberystwyth, where they have barely reached double
figures, but I don't think their autumn brochure is out yet.

Dawn King's agent is back from holiday tomorrow and we will
proceed with negotiations. Negotiations with Culture Project in
New York still trudge on. Not all our demands have been met,
and American Equity's ruling is expensive. The strength of our
position is reinforced by the fact that I shan't mind too much if
things do finally fall through. I don't really want to be in New
York for ten weeks; I would much rather be at Out of Joint
pestering you and finalising our plan of attack for 2013/14. I
look forward to seeing you again later this week.

I haven't been big on the Olympics, although I loved Danny's opening ceremony, but putting all the triumphalism aside I cannot but reflect that the formula proven in London this summer seems to have been: talent + funding = success. Funny, that. If there was a theatrical Olympics, Team GB would probably still top the medals table, but for how much longer? Thanks for the tip about Easter Island. I find Pacific cultures fascinating.

13th August 2012

Dear Max,

Thank you for inviting me to rehearsals on Tuesday. It was a great pleasure to witness Bill Gaskill take rehearsals and also to watch part of the play take shape. I think I said to you that I saw the original production at the Court way back when. I also worked with students on some of the scenes when I was teaching – so it is a play that I know reasonably well. I think that the political and humanitarian messages are as relevant as ever, and I hope that audiences respond to that as much as they did the first time.

Best wishes for rehearsals when you move to Bolton next week, and I look forward to seeing the production in London when it comes to St James Theatre.

19th August 2012

Dear Frank,

I've time for a quick letter before driving up to Bolton in half an hour. The experiment of having paying guests in rehearsal realised £825 and gave us sufficient experience to handle arrangements with even more dexterity next time. The actors are, I think, nonetheless relieved to have a week in Bolton of comparative privacy. We also sold £228 of books during this time, of which approximately £88 is profit for Out of Joint. The guests themselves were delighted by the experience and the response from them has been without exception enthusiastic and grateful. Most have also declared their intention of seeing the play itself either at Watford or at the St James.

On other fronts, Graham has secured the rights for Dawn King's play *Ciphers*, and I will address that when I return from Bolton. Negotiations with Culture Project may well be shipwrecked on the reef of American Equity's intransigence. As a penalty for including three English/Irish actors they still insist that the salaries of all ten actors should be raised from $425 to $970 per week. I think this makes the whole programme very doubtful. In Oxford, Naomi Jones (a former assistant) concluded a week's short workshop on verbatim theatre with a dozen students. Operated in conjunction with the Oxford Playhouse, this will generate a small profit. I will forward her report to you.

The advances for *Our Country's Good* continue to be strong (except for Aberystwyth where they are completely static).

Thank you for dropping in to rehearsal last week. Your continued interest is a source of great reassurance.

Generally speaking I enjoy the experience of touring, and it is fascinating to compare the political acumen of audiences in, say, Bolton or Liverpool, with the more middle-class appreciation of houses in Oxford or Southampton. At the same time, I love the wee home that Stella has made for us in Manor Gardens, and prolonged periods of absence, as was necessary while opening *Our Country's Good* in Bolton, are invariably followed by the great pleasures of returning home and indeed of reacquaintance with the comforting routine of the office.

28th August 2012

Dear Frank,

I am taking advantage of a return to London over the bank holiday weekend to write to you again. In fact, I increasingly find the amount of time necessarily involved in being away from home wearisome and enervating. However, as the great Samuel Johnson said, 'To be happy at home is the ultimate result of all ambition, the end to which every enterprise and labour tends.' In part, this tedium is balanced by the endless fascination of experiencing at first hand how another theatre organisation works, and here I must say that the staff at the Bolton Octagon from David Thacker downwards have been terrific hosts. The set has been beautifully made by their workshop and their enthusiasm and commitment to *Our Country's Good* have been heartening. For the last week we have been able to rehearse on the set, which will save a lot of time in the technical rehearsals next week. The play itself is beginning to look good although I still have a way to go in terms of both coherence and confidence. People will inevitably compare it with the productions I did in 1988 and 1998, but the truth is I can remember little about the detail of them. However, the important thing is that the play seems as bold and as brilliant as ever. One significant day in rehearsal came when we were visited by a young actor who had served three years for assault in a Belfast prison and who told us of acting in a prison production of Frank McGuinness's play *Observe the Sons of Ulster Marching Towards the Somme*. After leaving prison he went to drama school. 'The theatre changed my life completely,' he told us: a heartening endorsement of the central message of the play. I am sorry I won't be in Birmingham on the 26th to welcome your colleagues.

The advance continues to look very good everywhere except Aberystwyth which is beginning to be a matter of some concern. I enclose below a table which details the amount of paid attendances in each theatre as of Monday 20th August:

Bolton	3 weeks from 3rd September	4,715
Birmingham	1 week from 25th September	636
Aberystwyth	1 week from 2nd October	23
Cheltenham	1 week from 9th October	654
Southampton	1 week from 16th October	228
Oxford	1 week from 23rd October	401
The Hague	1 week from 30th October	304
Watford	1 week from 6th November	317
Leeds	2 weeks from 13th November	504
St James, London	6 weeks from 30th January	323

If this doesn't improve, Aberystwyth will seriously mar our 'subsidy per seat' record! The point I am making is that any touring company is a hostage to the efficiency and marketing policy of the venues we tour to. We have provided Aberystwyth with exactly the same marketing tools as every other theatre. Graham is always keen, as our annual report to you will confirm, to expand our touring by visiting new theatres. I was particularly enthusiastic about establishing a foothold in Wales with the Gareth Thomas project in mind, but is this boldness wise? From their brochure (only just arrived in proof form) I see that *Our Country's Good* is the only play in the Aberystwyth autumn season that is programmed for more than two nights. So this is clearly an innovative step for them too, but will this innovation be punished? I hope not. Incidentally, I heard on the radio that two-thirds of officers serving in the army describe themselves as being in 'a state of low morale' because of cuts in the defence budget. I am convinced that a survey of theatre practitioners would yield a similar result. The pressure you impose on us is, I fear, unremitting and relentless. I recall several productions at the Royal Court when the pressure to succeed was acute and particular, but with our output currently reduced to one play a year I have never felt more pressure to succeed at the box office than I do now with *Our Country's Good*.

17th September 2012

Dear Frank,

I may have addressed many of the points in our convivial and helpful meeting last week, but repetition is often a useful and necessary condition in the theatre. So I'm sure you will forgive me. I know I touched on the breadth and scope of our workshop programme and how by the end of January I will have conducted workshops in schools ranging from a Jesuit palace in the Lancashire Dales (Stonyhurst) to a Muslim girls school in the Commercial Road, E1 (Mulberry School) and a comprehensive in Reading. This programme enables us to contact a new generation of theatregoers as well as providing a small but useful stream of supplementary income. I think it would be hard to find another artistic director of any theatre company in the country who conducts more workshops in the course of a year.

We are implementing the new earning schemes in our business plan with determination. While I was in Bolton, my former Assistant Director, Naomi Jones, conducted a week-long workshop on verbatim theatre in conjunction with the Oxford Playhouse. I enclose her report [see Appendix 4]. This was aimed at first-time writers and will generate a small profit of £300. Out of Joint is also conducting a writing workshop with the Salisbury Playhouse aimed at first-time writers from the South West. This is being managed by Out of Joint's part-time Literary Manager, Sam Potter, and will involve me taking two day-long sessions with the seventeen aspirant writers. On 28th September we have an all-day inset day for fifteen teachers at Out of Joint. This is focused on *Our Country's Good,* and with the help of two actors who will come down from Birmingham and with Timberlake I will be directing three scenes from the play. The inset day is budgeted to earn Out of Joint just over £2,000 and the Salisbury Project £1,300. All this, together with the paid rehearsals, should be seen as a robust attempt to follow your bidding and diversify our income streams. The actors had rather more reservations about the visitors to rehearsal than I had realised at the time, and I will incorporate their thoughts in the end-of-term report that, as we agreed, will follow *Our Country's Good*. As I had anticipated, houses in Bolton have started to pick up following the notices and now that the schools are back. Attendances have averaged about 185 per performance in the two weeks so far, but I hope this figure will be much nearer 200 by the end of the run in Bolton next week. Advances continue to build steadily everywhere except Aberystwyth. I am hopeful that by the time your colleagues see it next week in Birmingham it will have accumulated that extra coat of varnish that only comes with success and the actors' knowledge that they are loved and cherished by the audience. Incidentally, rehearsal attendances yielded £825 and 86 people attended: many came twice and some came three times, and the final total was £330 of books sold over this time. To date we have 52 Friends, who have contributed £15,836. A two-week drive by my assistant Barney Norris targeted largely at agents just before I went into rehearsal for *Our Country's Good* netted over £3,000. The lesson here is that the Friends scheme doesn't expand by itself; it needs pretty constant attention.

Out of Joint have now secured the rights to Dawn King's *Ciphers*, and I have meetings planned with James Brining at the West Yorkshire Playhouse and with Vicky Featherstone at the Royal Court seeking co-production partnerships.

I went to two theatre openings this week which are worthy of comment. The new St James Theatre where *Our Country's Good* is to play in January is, I am told, the first purpose-built theatre to open in central London for thirty years. It looks very nice and will suit *Our Country's Good* well, but from the patchwork diversity of its programme it doesn't promise well as a long-term London partner for Out of Joint. The Bolton Octagon, on the other hand, has become very enthusiastic about our relationship, and we were urged to return by several patrons at the Investigate Day at Bolton last week, when there was a whole morning of discussion and rehearsal exercises run by David Thacker and myself.

The second opening was of Caryl Churchill's brilliant new play *Love and Information*. It has quite rightly garnered excellent reviews and much praise, but its experimental structure and lack of narrative drive move it into the 'threatening' area, and means it is very unlikely to be seen outside London. Does this matter? Does this concern the Arts Council, or are you happy to let market forces determine regional programming?

I look forward to hearing your colleagues' reaction to *Our Country's Good*.

I received no response to either of these points either.

In the past, Out of Joint's business model has been to seek co-production partnerships both with London and regional theatres. In 2011, Stella's play *Bang Bang Bang* had been a co-production with the Bolton Octagon, the Leicester Curve, the Salisbury Playhouse and the Royal Court as well as Out of Joint. This meant production costs could be shared and Out of Joint could offer new work of a nature and quality that a regional theatre might otherwise not have access to.

Simply reading about the amount of activity Out of Joint was involved in during the latter part of 2012 makes me exhausted! We were straining every sinew to raise money from any possible source. At the same time, Caryl Churchill took issue with the Royal Court for accepting sponsorship from Coutts bank for her production of *Love and Information* without prior consultation with her. It was a debate that had surfaced several times before in the Royal Court's history and is difficult to resolve. I think at this point Out of Joint would happily have accepted funding from Genghis Khan.

I never had much time for doing workshops in schools when I was at the Royal Court, but with Out of Joint they have become a major part of our operation. I conduct about thirty a year and my associate directors or Panda Cox (my former assistant, who then became Deputy Producer and Education Manager of Out of Joint) or Barney Norris, my assistant, take more. It provides Out of Joint with a small stream of subsidiary income and encourages teachers to book school parties. But above all it's fun. Usually the workshops are focused on the particular play currently in our repertoire, although there are many requests for workshops on *Our Country's Good* and *Top Girls* because they are on the school syllabus, as indeed am I, as a practitioner. I begin with games and some simple improvisations. These are aimed at breaking down the kids' inhibitions. We then do some status games with playing cards, and finally I focus on one scene from the particular play they have been studying. Any particular group has a pecking order determined by the values rated by that particular society. A group of convicts being transported to Australia may, for example, rate toughness, defiance, independence very highly, while a group of Year Twelve students might assess clothes, skill at games, friends or age as more important. To begin with I give playing cards at random and let the class find their own particular 'status' and place within a pecking order. Then I may place them in a particular situation, also giving them cards selected at random. For example, an office cleaner may have to clean an office within a particular and strict time limit, but the office might be needed by a banker who has to make a call to Hong Kong at a particular time. The outcome should be determined by the card, which, of course, could be very different from the role—the cleaner could pick a nine and the banker a three. My exercises are shamelessly purloined from Keith Johnstone, who worked with the Traverse Workshop Company when we were in the Theatre Upstairs in 1969, and who details his own working practices in his book *Impro*, and from various actors I have worked with over the years. I have been to Eton and Stonyhurst College as well as secondary moderns and what Alastair Campbell described as 'bog-standard comprehensives' all over the place. Doing actioning (the application of a transitive verb to a line, as explained in my previous books *Letters to George* and *Taking Stock*) is hard, because few kids know what a transitive verb is these days, but the real difference between an indifferent school and a good one is the presence of a committed and enthusiastic teacher. They can crop up anywhere.

I usually start with 'attitudes'. In the eighteenth century, on retirement, actors would publish a book of their favourite 'attitudes', which would depict the emotional content of a particular moment. There's a picture in the Theatre Museum by Reynolds which shows Garrick doing 'Is this a dagger I see before me?' from *Macbeth*. His attitude is 'terror'. Premiership footballers have developed quite complex and individual 'attitudes' to celebrate a goal, and Gareth Thomas vividly illuminated his particular attitude of 'joy' in the workshop we conducted with him at Bridgend College. It consisted of running in small circles while slapping the top of his fearsomely shaven pate. Since he scored forty-one times for Wales I guess he had plenty of opportunity to finesse this 'attitude'.

I use cards to play status games and then extend the use of cards to signify what Stanislavsky would have called the specific of a scene. A good one for students is a bus-stop scene where two students, one male, one female, are given two cards at random. The cards indicate their attraction to each other. The inhibitions flee, and testosterone flows! Kids are unerringly canny at reading each other's body language, and they invariably perceive the attraction each has for the other, while I am often left mystified.

Occasionally I use transgressive games to assess and discover the emotional weight of an argument. One of these is 'The Fucking Game', although Stella only lets me do that with older students. In this game any actor can introduce the word 'fucking' into the dialogue to emphasise their passion and the argument, so the first rehearsal scene in *Our Country's Good* might become:

RALPH. Good afternoon ladies and gentlemen.

DABBY. We're ladies now. Wait till I tell my fucking husband
    I've become a fucking lady.

MARY. Sssht.

RALPH. It is with pleasure that I welcome you.

SIDEWAY. Our pleasure Mr Clark, our pleasure.

RALPH. We have many days of hard work ahead of us.

LIZ. I'm not fucking working, I thought we was fucking acting.

And so on.

Allowing kids to break the taboo of bad language can have unexpected results. One assessment form came back from a school in Hertfordshire: 'I thought the workshop was fucking great,' it said.

24th September 2012

Dear Frank,

The good news is that, as I suspected, attendances have surged for *Our Country's Good* in the final week of its run in Bolton. Every performance except Monday the number of paying punters was over 300. I will send final figures next week when we have subtracted the complimentary tickets and worked out an average attendance per performance figure. Aberystwyth continues to be a concern and the advance in Southampton is a bit disappointing, but otherwise advances are building well.

Blanche McIntyre has accumulated a string of awards and excellent reviews, notably for her productions of *Foxfinder* (another play by Dawn King) and *Accolade*, a revival of a 1950 play by Emlyn Williams, and I have asked her to direct *Ciphers*. We are now in the process of setting up co-production arrangements for autumn 2013. The downside of this is that we will not be doing a further production in the coming calendar year, and I will not be going into rehearsal again till the 30th December 2013 at the earliest. This gap of sixteen months between productions will be the longest I have ever experienced since starting work at the Royal Court in 1979 and must be regarded as a sad but inevitable waste of Out of Joint's resources. It is, however, an incentive to make *Dr Johnson* and *The Seagull* happen in New York. This is now to be marketed as a Tribute to Max Stafford-Clark Season, which is very flattering, but as I wrote in an earlier letter I don't much want to spend ten weeks in New York; I would far rather be tending Out of Joint, but this too is forced upon me by circumstances. Allan Buchman is coming to London next weekend, and I hope the contractual arrangements will then at last be finalised.

Usually in the annual assessment we are asked to point to the achievement of which the company is most proud in the preceding year. Graham and I would unhesitatingly point to *Bang Bang Bang* which, among its other virtues, is a classic Royal Court/Out of Joint/'other worlds' play revealing the details of and giving access to the complexities of a world unknown to the audience. I believe passionately in the value and worth of this work, and it saddens me to think that it will be more than two years between *Bang Bang Bang* and the next opportunity Out of Joint will have to undertake a similar project. The missing £100,000 would enable us to make fuller use of my time and to exploit Out of Joint's resources properly. You know it makes sense!

The reading of *This May Hurt A Bit,* Stella Feehily's NHS play, is scheduled for 3 p.m. on Friday 26th October at the National Theatre Studio.

I am inordinately proud of *Bang Bang Bang*, and when students ask, as they do occasionally, 'What is your favourite production ever?', I would, for the moment, reply that it was *Bang Bang Bang*. The truth is that productions merge into the past and I can only remember favourite moments: Donal McCann's unflinching and unbearably moving performance at the end of Sebastian Barry's *The Steward of Christendom*; the stunning and unexpected standing ovation at the end of the first preview of *Our Country's Good*; the terrifying muscled soldiers frisking and harassing the audience as they tried to enter *Macbeth*; or Ian Dury's obscene anthem at the end of the first half of Caryl Churchill's *Serious Money*. But *Bang Bang Bang* is recent enough for me to remember it whole. It began like a number of other Out of Joint productions with a two-week workshop (in 2008), in which we met NGO workers, doctors, government officials, academics, human rights defenders and journalists who had worked in the Democratic Republic of Congo (DRC). We found a designer, the incredibly talented Miriam Nabarro, who had worked in the DRC for a year with a Dutch NGO called Warchild. One of the most striking people we met was Anneke von Woudenberg, a senior researcher for Human Rights Watch who had worked in the Congo over a number of years. Her specific job was to gather evidence against war criminals. She had given up a £250,000 salary in the City to work for Oxfam. She described a meeting with one particularly frightening and notorious warlord. Blonde and very attractive, she owned that she made full use of her femininity, changing into high heels and touching up her lippy before her encounter in the jungle. Once rehearsals started in 2011 I contacted her again and she came into rehearsal where she sportingly took part in an improvisation in which she interviewed the play's warlord, Colonel Mburame, as played by Babou Ceesay. It was enormously instructive, and Babou was indeed properly intimidated. The play began with the terrifying assault of a young French human rights defender, based on an account we were given. At its best, Out of Joint's work is educative and reveals another world to both audiences and participants; in the course of the last twenty years I have learned how to cook crack cocaine, how to deliver a baby, how to set up a hedge fund and how to assemble an AK47.

In the early eighties I produced a play by Robert Holman called *Other Worlds* at the Royal Court. It had Jim Broadbent and Juliet Stevenson in the cast and was beautifully designed by John Byrne and luminously directed by Richard Wilson. But Jim and Juliet were not yet stars, and *Other Worlds* played to what I imagine to be still a Royal

Court box-office record; one night there were just five paying punters in an auditorium which can seat four hundred. Some years later when I was about to leave the Court I undertook a production of *The Recruiting Officer*. Wishing to emulate the intimacy of Restoration drama I restored the side-boxes at the Royal Court, which in the intervening years had become downstage entrances and lighting positions respectively. However, our newly acquired box-office computer was unable to digest these additions... so the four boxes acquired names from the Royal Court's illustrious past to help the front-of-house staff allocate and identify them. One was called *Look Back in Anger*, another *Saved*, a third was *Tom and Viv*, a nod to the one commercial success I had done in my time at the Court, and I canvassed the staff to suggest names for the fourth. 'I reckon we should call it *Other Worlds*, guv,' said the long-serving master carpenter, Chris Harding-Roberts. I pointed out that this had hardly been one of the Royal Court's most glorious moments. 'No, but it's what we do, isn't it, other worlds,' replied Chris.

He was right, of course. And *Bang Bang Bang* was a classic 'other worlds' play. One unwavering imperative for both verbatim work and any kind of researched piece is that, though one may know the general direction, it's important to remain undecided about the final destination until the last possible moment, remaining open to the discoveries of rehearsal. So in *Bang Bang Bang* Stella had started the workshop enthusiastic about a 'work hard, play hard' culture wherein young people were saving lives by day but snorting coke by night. There was a hilarious party in the final script, but the purpose and integrity of the people we had met, like Anneke, took the play in a different direction.

4th October 2012

Dear Frank,

The big news is that *Our Country's Good* continues to perform well. The few notices we have had are excellent (5 stars in the *Morning Star*, 4 stars in the *Guardian*, the

Telegraph and the *Mail*), and the local reviews are very good too. I enclose a selection of them. I believe the standard both of ensemble acting and the values of the supporting production (lighting, design, direction) to be extremely high. But then I would, wouldn't I! I'm thrilled with the response, but more importantly I'm delighted with the work itself, even if I sometimes feel as if I'm stuck in an eighties time warp! I look forward to learning the responses of your colleagues who saw it in Birmingham. Apart from the Saturday matinee, houses were all over 300 in Birmingham and the cast are very happy. However, I fear Aberystwyth next week may be a sobering experience for them.

On Friday 28th September we conducted an inset day at Out of Joint for nineteen teachers. Lisa Kerr and Ian Redford came down from Birmingham, Timberlake talked about the genesis of the play, and a teacher from the King Alfred School in Hampstead who had taught the play for fifteen years talked about the approaches examiners took to the play. I asked the teachers for a written response on the day, which I will pass on to you in my end-of-tour report. Out of Joint made a 'profit' of £1,874 from the inset day. This certainly provides an incentive to set up a second day, possibly in January or February. One unsettling fact to emerge from the day was the disappointment of a number of the teachers that their schools could no longer afford £150 for a two-hour workshop. This is an income stream that may have been dammed. On Saturday 29th I had a three-hour meeting with our producer Karl Sydow and Allan Buchman, and we made an agreement to present the Out of Joint production *Dr Johnson* in New York, and for me to direct *The Seagull*. As I wrote to you earlier I don't much want to be away for so long, but this too will provide Out of Joint with some supplementary income.

I will send properly annotated figures from Bolton and Birmingham on my return from Wales.

PS. The correct paid attendance per night in Birmingham was 261: somewhat better than our self-appointed target of 200 ppn but rather less than the 300 I had set my heart on.

The week in Aberystwyth turned out to be a highlight of the tour; audiences were far better than I had feared, Stella and I found a lovely bed and breakfast on the seafront and, most delightful of all, on the Wednesday morning I took the whole company on the beautiful Vale of Rheidol Railway from Aberystwyth up to Devil's Bridge. The leaves were just turning and the ride up the valley was spectacular. The theatre itself is situated on the campus, and the audiences were young and enthusiastic. The discovery of an excellent Spanish tapas bar in the town also did much to boost company morale.

11th October 2012

Dear Frank,

Aberystwyth wasn't the desolate disaster I had feared. Attendances will be short of our target 200, but there were 260 on the first night, 180 to 190 on most nights thereafter, dipping to 95 on Thursday. There were standing ovations on two nights, and the response forms, which I will summarise in my end-of-term report, ranged from the positive to the ecstatic. The company found it a very worthwhile experience, and it is good to have had such a positive reaction in a venue that is new to us, but nonetheless it won't do much for our 'subsidy per seat' performance this year. I mentioned this to you in my letter of 28th August and would appreciate a response. One frustration is that, though the *Guardian* and the *Telegraph* have given us exuberant reviews, they have only appeared online and have not been printed in the paper itself.

I know from your background that you are familiar with touring, but it is worth going over the details of our arrival in a new theatre to emphasise how much work goes into maintaining standards of excellence. The set is trucked from the previous venue (in this case Birmingham) on Sunday, and the get-in starts on Monday morning. On Monday evening I check lighting states and positions with the relighter (after a six-hour train journey to Aberystwyth) and we commence a three-hour technical rehearsal with the actors at 2 p.m. on Tuesday. The show is followed by brief and speedy technical notes and a forty-minute post-show discussion. After which we sell £142 worth of books. On Wednesday at 11 a.m. I do a two-hour workshop with students from five different local secondary schools. [I then catch the 3.30 p.m. train from Aberystwyth and after a breakdown outside Shrewsbury and a missed connection in Birmingham arrive home just in time for the 10 o'clock news: a thirteen-hour day!]

Workshops are an area of concern. Despite the pessimism of the teachers recorded in last week's letter there continues to be an overwhelming demand for this particular play, as *Our Country's Good* is on the syllabus. I am able to undertake only about two workshops a week, which places a burden on Panda, Des, Barney and even on the actors themselves to lead workshops. I am unable to monitor this with the attention I would ideally desire, and my concern is about maintaining the standard and focus we have set. We make a 'profit' of about £80 per workshop so the financial incentive is not huge, despite our determination to maximise all sources of income.

I enclose a table which will give you some indication of how our business plan is working out in practice. Column 1 gives the income last year (2011/12) from all sources other than the box-office revenue and Arts Council funding. Column 2 is the budgeted prediction for 2012/13 taken from the business plan. Column 3 is the actual figure for 2012/13. Our income from the Friends scheme was boosted this week by a generous cheque from Richard Bean. Stella and I had dinner with Danny Boyle, our other generous benefactor, this week. He fears that, now the government realise that investment in sport leads to excellent results and consequent popularity, there will be pressure to move money from Arts and Culture (unpopular) to Sport (popular). I fear he may be right.

Other Earned Income	2011/12	2012/13 Original Business Plan	2012/13 Actual
Education			
Workshops	£3,959	£1,240	£4,654
Literary Workshops		£1,300	£37
Inset Days		£2,560	£2,847
Universities		£400	£2,800
Summer Schools		£1,550	£356
Open Rehearsals			£858
Fundraising (Friends Scheme and Donations)	£5,200	£8,800	£27,907
Management Fees			£663
Book Sales	£12,092	£4,020	£6,894
Rehearsal Room	£3,752	£6,000	£7,533
TOTAL	**£25,003**	**£25,870**	**£47,486**

Our desperate attempts to maximise our income from other sources was having some success, although we had overestimated the amount we would get from workshops and the summer school in Oxford, while travel costs absorbed most of the income from Salisbury. The Friends scheme had produced far more income than I had anticipated, but a substantial amount had been in one-off donations that would not be repeated in subsequent years. The floodgates of generosity were opened by the donors' outrage at the Arts Council cut—also an effect which will not be repeated. Well, I hope not!

15th October 2012

Dear Frank,

There continues to be good news. *Our Country's Good* played to over 600 paying punters on Tuesday night in Cheltenham and figures for the whole week have continued to be buoyant with many 'Bravos', and a couple of standing ovations. It's not really for me to say that I think the work is 'excellent' – although I certainly do – but 'excellence' or 'excellent' is a word used no fewer than 23 times in your pamphlet 'Achieving Great Art for Everyone', so it is clearly a quality you have trumpeted loudly and that you will champion and support. I'm glad to hear it.

It is, however, another aspect of 'Achieving Great Art for Everyone' that I would like to focus on. Education workshops have always been an integral part of Out of Joint's core mission, but they are beginning to be an area of concern. Last week Panda did a workshop in a girls' school in West Kirby outside Liverpool. Effectively this took up her whole day and the travel costs very nearly outweighed any 'profit' from the trip. Your manifesto clearly states 'We will invest in arts practice produced for children and young people', and again, 'We will give young people access to excellent art'. In another place the pamphlet states, 'We will broker partnerships with other public and private funders to secure greater impact...'

Well, how about it? Our education workshops need brokering or they may well be broke. For a comparatively small sum we would be able to cap the fee for workshops, thus making them yet more accessible, and we could also train a team of workshop leaders to cover all the requests we receive. This will refresh and augment our existing commitment to young people, which is absolutely in line with one of the Arts Council's principal goals. Could I have a response on this please?

I apologise for not being able to get you accurate figures for the run in Bolton but the new box-office technology continues to outwit their staff there, and Jon Bradfield has been on holiday for the last week. I believe the final figure will be around 220. This is more than the 180 for *Mixed Up North* (a new play with strong local connections) and the 140 for *Bang Bang Bang* (a 'threatening' new play), but rather less than I would have expected for an esteemed modern classic. Interestingly, attendance actually dropped on Saturday nights when no student tickets or other concessions were available. This does seem to bear out my theory that regional audiences peaked around 2005/06 and that there is manifest and considerable resistance to higher price levels.

The figures I sent you in the table last week are already redundant. An extraordinarily generous cheque from Alan Rickman has taken the figure for Friends and Donations to £24,151 – beyond our revised estimate of £19,500 and some way above the £8,800 of the original business plan. However, £16,000 of this sum total is from six generous individuals who won't take kindly to further requests next year. I fear it will be much harder to reach £20,000 next year. Another figure that happily needs adjusting is that for book sales: the £12,092 for 2011/12 includes programme sales while the 2012/13 figures do not.

Meanwhile, we are continuing to forge contacts with associate universities and also expand our provision of literary workshops. I will report back on the pilot scheme with the Salisbury Playhouse once it is concluded in December.

So, in conclusion, for a little more money we could spread a great deal more 'excellence'. Isn't that what you want?

22nd October 2012

Dear Frank,

This is the sixth letter I have written to you since our meeting on 13th September [again there was no reply] and although I understand that you have an onerous workload and are unable to reply every week, I would appreciate some response… particularly to the points made about our education workshops in my last letter. We have many hundreds of glowing assessment forms accumulated from each of the theatres we visit. Fundraising continues energetically and the Friends and Donations scheme now stands at £25,201, swelled by a cheque from Sir Ian McKellen last week. My reservations about this being a long-term source of revenue remain however.

I am looking forward to the workshop next week for *This May Hurt A Bit* at the National Theatre Studio. The reading is now at 2 p.m. at the Studio on Friday the 26th. We have had a traumatic week recasting as Nigel Planer dropped out because his father is ill and Stephanie Cole has also had to go to hospital herself.

I am reinstituting the Critics' Lunch we used to hold annually at the Royal Court, and Karl Sydow will host a lunch at the Garrick Club before Christmas. This will give me an opportunity to brief them about the necessity for our rather conservative programming decisions and also to comment on the threat that the cuts make to our ability to take creative risks. It will be a jolly occasion. We will play party games, and they will each have to plan two years' work for Out of Joint within current budget restrictions.

Dr Johnson and *The Seagull* both appear to be happening in New York, although the final Equity hurdle has not yet been cleared. I shall believe it when I'm on the plane!

It transpired that Frank responded to hectoring with greater alacrity than he did to attempts to nudge him into any more convivial form of conversation—my plaintive demand for a reply bore fruit the very next day.

23rd October 2012

Dear Max,

Thank you for your six letters in as many weeks. I take that as an indicator of an enhanced level of fondness that you have for us.

I have been spending some time investigating how I could most helpfully respond to your request in last week's letter about the issues that you have been experiencing with workshops. I hope some of the below helps.

Firstly, I of course have sympathy with your situation. I have spoken to colleagues who confirmed what I suspected to be the case – that is, that this is a very common situation with education/workshop providers around the country – not just for theatre practitioners, or indeed arts and culture practitioners, but more widely. The context for education spending, teacher time, priorities and many other factors mean that there is a fairly difficult climate to be operating in and many organisations are in a similar position to you, if not worse. You, at least have a very strong USP, a strong track record and a number of contacts.

Just to be clear, though, 'brokering partnerships with other funders' means with respect to funding programmes – for example, our joint NESTA Digital Fund or working with the Dept of Education for Music Education Hubs or the DCMS/HLF jointly funded Catalyst programme. It does not mean between individual arts/cultural organisations and other funders. We don't have the skills or the capacity to do this; even if we did, it would risk all sorts of conflict between the hundreds of organisations we fund. Having said that, I recently emailed Graham telling him that the Catalyst 3 programme (for building fundraising capacity) is due to be launched, all being well, next Monday. This is aimed at organisations with limited or no fundraising experience to fund capacity-building around fundraising. We are anticipating that there will be a lot of interest in this programme and consequently it will be quite competitive; however, I would have thought that Out of Joint are in a position to be able to put together a strong application.

As I indicated before, we are looking at joint applications from more than one organisation. Perhaps Out of Joint could consider working with someone with an education background. We are anticipating that deadlines for applications will be the end of January which should give you time to scope out possible partners, should you so wish.

Something else that may be of interest is a piece of commissioned research project into London schools' cultural engagement. Over the past eighteen months, Arts Council and the GLA have supported AND in the associated dialogue. This research activity itself was made possible through the legacy of the Working with Children's Services (Capital Ambition) project, project-managed by the MLA and delivered in partnership with Arts Council, London. This has been a crucial piece of research for AND in their Bridge role. National Foundation for Education Research (NFER) have led on this research. The final report can be read via this link:
www.nfer.ac.uk/nfer/publications/ANDL02/ANDL02.pdf

I hope that you and/or Panda find some of the above useful.

I am pleased to see that you are making good progress with your business plan targets around other earned income; also, that *Our Country's Good* continues to perform well (even in Aberystwyth!). I am planning to see the show in Watford, but I haven't as yet booked myself a ticket. I will let you know when I am going.

I am very much looking forward to the reading on Friday – although, of course, I am very sorry to hear about Nigel Planer and Stephanie Cole.

Look forward to seeing you then.

There was an offer of a free badge, which was enticing, but though Frank clearly intended to be helpful, the hoops we had to jump through, and acronyms we were urged to decipher, were bewildering.

*

The week of the 22nd October was spent at the National Theatre Studio workshopping Stella's play *This May Hurt A Bit*. This was very different to either the *Witches* workshop with Rebecca Lenkiewicz or the Gareth Thomas workshop largely because there was a script. In 2008, Stella and I had had an initial exploratory workshop, also at the Studio, during which we had interviewed doctors, nurses, patients, hospital porters, hospital administrators, journalists, GPs, surgeons, bed managers, health-service academics and politicians. In the intervening four years Stella had digested this material and written a script. (I had also been thoughtful enough to provide her with first-hand experience through my six months as a guest of the NHS—and yes, I did have a bed next to an incontinent vicar, poor man, who has found his way into Stella's play.) The objective of the week was to test out the script, a process which would conclude with a public reading on the Friday afternoon, principally for members of the NT's literary team. The majority of the cast were Out of Joint alumni: David Rintoul (*Andersen's English*), Nigel Cooke (*Dreams of Violence*), Matthew Needham (*Our Country's Good*), Brian Protheroe (*The Convict's Opera*), Niamh Cusack (*Andersen's English*), Susan Engel (the *Witches* workshop) and Karina Fernandez (*The Convict's Opera*). They were joined by Lorna Brown, who was doing a play at the National Theatre at the time, and Julian Wadham, another veteran comrade of mine who had been in the first production of *Our Country's Good* alongside *The Recruiting Officer*, and several other shows, including *Falkland Sound*, during my time at the Royal Court. The cast was completed by Neil Kinnock. Neil's presence needs some explanation: Stella's play begins with a spirited dialogue about the National Health Service between Aneurin Bevan and Winston Churchill. Neil had been brought up in the same Welsh village as Bevan (Tredegar). On one occasion, naughty Neil, then underage, had been drinking with friends in a local pub when Bevan and Jenny Lee walked in. Bevan bought them all a drink while Lee phoned

Neil's mother to tell her what her son was up to! Neil was a terrific addition to the cast, who grew very fond and protective of him as the week progressed, as did he of them. We were regaled with some very high-level political gossip, and he brought a particular energy and charisma to the workshop, not to mention an expertise to Bevan's House of Commons speech which launched the NHS, and which Stella had taken and edited from Hansard. He argued a bit, and I found myself saying on one occasion, 'Neil, you'll never be an actor unless you learn to take a note.' The fact that he had no particular desire or ambition to be an actor at all temporarily eluded me. Stella's play is not a documentary, not a family drama, not a farce, not a verbatim piece and not a polemic, although it contains elements of all these. It needed particularly deft and agile playing as the play slipped from one mode to another. We had a terrific week, the cast surpassed themselves on the Friday afternoon, and Neil's speech as Bevan brought the play to an appropriately unexpected and stirring climax. Above all, the week had shown Stella her script and prompted her in the direction of various developments and refinements. She now has three months to finalise a delivery draft which was to be scrutinised by Nick Hytner and the National's Literary Manager, Sebastian Born. The downside is that the Cottesloe is to be closed for the whole of 2013, so it will not be till summer 2014 at the earliest that *This May Hurt A Bit* will reach the public if it were to be at the National.

5th November 2012

Dear Frank,

Our Country's Good first. The week in The Hague was much enjoyed by the cast. Audiences were round the 200 mark. However, despite the universal excellence of English there was a tangible cultural slippage from the Dutch audience, as their response was not quite as effusive as the actors had come to expect from our regional British audiences. Nonetheless both the British and the Australian Ambassadors were particularly enthusiastic, and both reiterated that it was the most exciting theatrical event in Holland for some years. Paid attendances at Aberystwyth numbered 195 per performance; way ahead of my worst fears and very creditable considering the small advance. Your assessor's report reached me last week; her only reservation was that the performances had 'not bedded down yet'. Since she saw the third performance in Bolton, the comment is perfectly just. However, a full state of 'bedded down-ness' was well achieved by Birmingham, and I look forward to hearing the reactions of your colleagues who saw it there, and indeed your own reaction when you see it in Watford this week. Such is the impact of *Our Country's Good* that often people have an iconic and treasured memory of their first experience of it and don't wish this precious remembrance to be disturbed by a fresh production.

We now have 53 Friends and have raised £25,701, boosted by a generous cheque from Dominic Cooke last week; it is notable that the heartland of our support comes from right across the theatrical community itself. Nonetheless, it is with a heavy heart that Graham and I laboured through the Catalyst 3 document. We will of course apply our minds to assembling a consortium, targeting individual donations (which as you know we have already had success with) and so on, and Graham will be asking your advice about various aspects of it. But it seems that instead of creating 'Great Art for Everyone' we must now transform ourselves into 'Not Very Great Fundraisers' in an effort to relieve the Arts Council of its own responsibilities. It is not much of an incentive to learn that no funds may be devoted to any artistic purpose. The terms of the document also prevent us forming a consortium with any of the universities or educational contacts we have already made, since they are not recipients of Arts Council funding.

On a more cheerful note I was delighted that you were able to come to the reading of *This May Hurt A Bit* last week. I thought it was a remarkable success, not least in that it spurred Stella in the direction of various enhancements and details. She now has three months to complete a delivery draft. The National will then make a judgement, but the news from all our co-producers is not good. The RSC have no possible slot for *Pitcairn* until late 2013 or more likely spring 2014. The National Theatre of Wales similarly have no funds for the Gareth Thomas project until 2014/15. And the NT have no slot until the summer of 2014. All of which puts us very firmly 'on hold'. I am however having a meeting with James Brining of the West Yorkshire Playhouse on the 14th November and will endeavour to persuade him to agree to a co-production of *Ciphers* in autumn 2013. All the other co-producers are, of course, waiting for further drafts before declaring their interest. I don't think we have much chance of persuading Lord Kinnock to take up an acting career so you may have witnessed what will prove to have been a truly unique and very special occasion!

I look forward to your reaction to *Our Country's Good*; I do hope you enjoy it.

The Catalyst 3, Tier 4 Funding Agreement needs some explanation; regularly funded companies, which, of course, includes Out of Joint, were announced eligible to apply for additional funding to train ourselves as fundraisers. We couldn't employ a fundraiser to raise funds with this additional money; that would not be sustainable. We could, however, employ a fundraiser to teach us how to raise funds. It was strictly prohibited to use any money from this source on productions themselves, or any production-related activity. We had to combine with another, or preferably three other companies, to form an application consortium, and these companies had to have been in receipt of regular Arts Council funding, so educational partners like schools or universities were ruled out. It was clear that the Arts Council were endeavouring to help us to help ourselves, but the strictures, rules and timing involved were incredibly convoluted.

12th November 2012

Dear Frank,

Our Country's Good continues to perform well at Watford, with the stage-management reports rating the audience at over 400 for every performance, although once again this figure dropped on Friday and Saturday in part because there are no schools bookings on those days. Andrew Russell, Arts Council East regional member, wrote on Twitter: '*Our Country's Good* is a moving, sharply acted, surprisingly funny, beautiful staging of a classic'. But I eagerly await your own response. Different teams have been busy giving workshops to schools although, ominously, we have had three cancellations in the course of the last week. In each case the headmaster vetoed the drama teacher's application for a workshop on budgetary grounds. I had hoped that the Tier 3 Catalyst scheme would help with this vital aspect of Out of Joint's operation, but it's hard to see any solace coming from that direction. This is one unequivocally successful part of Out of Joint's operation, and it is staggering through lack of funding. We clearly can't charge more – nor are we in a position to charge less, or we will be running our workshops at a loss. I am unable to believe that the Arts Council, with its proclaimed commitment to education and young people, is unable to help. We have many testimonials of the value of our workshops to both teachers and pupils, which will follow in my end-of-term report.

The final figure for paying punters per night at Oxford was 389, and it is salutary to compare this to the figure for Oxford for the 1998 production, which was 520. This would seem to bear out my theory that regional audiences for new work peaked around 2005.

We have approached the Lyric Hammersmith to join us in a Catalyst consortium, and once again I emphasise how desperately we need help to maintain our commitment to education work.

It was clear by the autumn of 2012 that it wasn't simply Out of Joint that was in distress. *The Stage* reported that a number of companies had ceased trading, and that many regional repertory theatres were in desperately vulnerable positions. Nick Hytner showed exemplary leadership of the theatre community at this point, and convened a well-publicised press conference at the National Theatre.

19th November 2012

Dear Frank,

I was delighted that the spirited and vital defence of regional theatre last week was led by two of my former assistants, Danny Boyle and Gemma Bodinetz. Danny cited his seminal experiences of regional theatre touring with Joint Stock's *Ragged Trousered Philanthropists* and *Cloud Nine*. Maria Miller, the current Culture Secretary, has been quoted as saying that theatres have got to get better at asking. Emboldened by this I intend to write and ask her for a meeting at which I shall lay out the crisis in our threatened education programme.

The final leg of our autumn tour of *Our Country's Good* opened last week at the West Yorkshire Playhouse. Houses have been good (over the 200 mark), and the response extremely enthusiastic. We have assiduously distributed assessment forms to the audiences, and I have also asked the actors to each write a report of their experience of the rehearsal process and the tour. I will collate and summarise these and pass this on to you in my end-of-term report, which I will start on next week. My meeting with James Brining went well, and although he stopped short of making a commitment to *Ciphers*, his enthusiasm about a co-production with Out of Joint was considerable. I have also sent the play to Ed Hall at Hampstead and to Madani Younis at the Bush, and am hopeful that one of them will step forward to be our London partner.

And now back to education. Your brochure 'Achieving Great Art for Everyone' bursts with enthusiasm for young people and the potency of making experience of theatre available to them. It is, as you confirm, at the centre of the Arts Council's mission. 'The arts are crucial to a holistic education that values creativity and nurtures talent.' Goal 5 is that 'every child and young person has the opportunity to experience the richness of the arts'. And, even more to the point, 'we will champion high-quality opportunities for children and young people to enjoy the arts in and out of school'. And finally, 'success will be more young people having access to excellent art'. By extension therefore, failure must be fewer young people having access to excellent art, and it is precisely this failure that concerns me and to which I will endeavour to draw Maria Miller's attention. To summarise, we have a popular and very successful programme of education workshops focused at the moment on a play, *Our Country's Good*, central to the school syllabus. The fee or charge for a two-hour workshop has slowly risen in increments from £120 in 1993 to £150 in 2008, since when it has been frozen. This is not an excessive increase but it has become increasingly clear that this price is now beyond the budgetary resources of many schools. On the one hand we need to train more workshop leaders to meet the increased demand brought by *Our Country's Good*, and at the same time we need to lower the fee to give young people the access that your brochure proclaims so valuable. 'We will champion high-quality opportunities' are ringing and inspiring sentiments, and I call on you to give them substance. So far in 2012/13 our workshop activity (22 two-hour workshops) has kept pace with our output in 2011/12 (22 two-hour workshops), and we have desperate need of a relatively modest amount to complete this financial year. We need a training day in which we train and empower six workshop leaders (this would cost £400), and we need to cap the remaining workshops of the year (estimated at 12) to a fee of £100 (which would cost £600). So – for the pitiful sum of £1,000 we can extend an enormously successful part of our operation and fulfil one of the Arts Council's principal goals. I simply do not believe that the Arts Council don't have the resources to 'champion' this programme, but I do fear that you may not have the will. Please prove me wrong.

There was no further response on the subject of education from Frank Endwright, or from anybody else at the Arts Council. It seemed they were prepared to spend a considerable sum trumpeting their purported achievements in education, but had no small change for investing therein. I sent Frank the end-of-term report that covered the tour of *Our Country's Good*. This was not a 'requirement' from the Arts Council, but I was determined to be both scrupulous and candid.

26th November 2012

Dear Frank,

I enclose the first instalment of the Endwright Report. Most of the actors have yet to send me their assessments but I will summarise them in the second instalment. Final figures for nightly paid attendances were:

Bolton	223
Birmingham	261
Aberystwyth	195
Cheltenham	257
Southampton	208
Oxford	359
The Hague	229
Watford	351
Leeds	241
Average (before Leeds)	258

Some comparisons with previous productions follow:

Production *figures in italics are lower than the specific PPN for this production*	Bolton	South-ampton	Oxford	Leeds
2012 (*Our Country's Good*)	**223**	**208**	**359**	**241**
2012 (*Top Girls*)			407	252
2011 (*Bang Bang Bang*)	*140*	*109*		
2010 (*Big Fella*)		*108*	*187*	
2010 (*Andersen's English*)				251
2009 (*Mixed Up North*)	*184*	*196*		
2009 (*Dreams of Violence*)		*159*		
2009 (*The Convict's Opera*)		246		*226*
2008 (*Testing the Echo*)			*107*	
2007 (*King of Hearts*)			*240*	
2006 (*The Overwhelming*)		*178*		*136*
2005 (*Talking to Terrorists*)		*158*	*215*	*156*
2003 (*The Permanent Way*)			535	344
2003 (*Duck*)				*199*
2002 (*She Stoops…/A Laughing Matter*)			*327*	
2001 (*Feelgood*)			470	
2000 (*Rita, Sue…/A State Affair*)			*186*	
1998 (*Our Country's Good*)			520	
1998 (*Our Lady of Sligo*)			536	
1997 (*Blue Heart*)			294	215
1996 (*Shopping and Fucking*)				*138*
1994 (*The Positive Hour*)			485	307

I'm not sure where this will leave our 'subsidy per seat' ratio. Obviously these figures are good, but with less subsidy and many fewer performances than last year I can't even speculate on the final ratio.

We have had a meeting with Polly Teale of Shared Experience to explore the possibilities of forming a Catalyst consortium with them, but our own fundraising has drooped in recent weeks as I have nearly run through all the Friendly names in my address book, and, of course, we are no nearer attracting sponsorship as none of us have the expertise to approach that world.

Workshop bookings continue to accumulate and I impatiently await your response to my request in that direction. Culture Project's appeal to American Equity upon which the whole programme of *A Dish of Tea with Dr Johnson* and *The Seagull* hinges will be heard 'after Thanksgiving and before the end of November', so hopefully that will be resolved soon. Also Trinity College Dublin are applying to various academic sources on our behalf to expedite the one night's performance we have arranged in the Provost's House.

I know Graham has a phone call arranged with you on the 27th and I look forward to hearing about that, and your views on *Our Country's Good*. The most unlikely piece of news is that I have been asked to take some rehearsal sessions for a school in Essex who are rehearsing *Talking to Terrorists*. The drama teacher told me she wanted to choose something unusual and challenging; so even Out of Joint's most 'threatening' plays are sometimes recycled by students!

30th November 2013

Dear Max,

Thank you for your recent letters.

It was a pleasure to watch *Our Country's Good*. As you may remember I saw the 1988 (or thereabouts) version at the Royal Court, and I was unsure how it would seem watching it again nearly a quarter of a century later. I thought the script has aged (matured?) remarkably well and the issues are at least as pertinent now as they were. It's obviously quite word-heavy, and I could imagine a production being leaden. However, I thought this production felt fresh and urgent. The staging and the energy and commitment of the performers pulled it along. I thought it had pace and brio. I'm very glad I saw it.

I spoke, albeit very briefly, with Panda after the reading at the NT Studio. She seemed very pleased with the information that I had forwarded to her and you about various education-related activities/networks, etc. She said that is going to follow some of those through. Many of our NPOs [National Portfolio Organisations, the Arts Council acronym for things they regularly fund rather than organisations funded on a project-by-project basis] and museums have education/CYP activities [this presumably means Children and Young People, though Frank does not elaborate – is he trying to blind me with science, or is this what working to the Arts Council does to the mind?] and some obviously have these as their entire *raison d'être*. They are funded wholly or in part to do this. Those programmes and our investment in those are the ways that we are investing in education-related work; we do not have any other programme or further funds to support this. Sadly, that means that there is no mechanism for you to apply for further funds to support the education work such as you mention. It may be worth repeating that there is far, far more valuable work that we would love to be able to support than we have the resources to do so. Our grant from government was cut by 30% last time; we only passed on 15% to the RFO/NPO [Regularly Funded Organisation/National Portfolio Organisation – the previous and current snakeskin in which we are bound] portfolio but that meant hacking back on the programmes. Our next DCMS [Department of Culture, Media and Sport] settlement is almost certainly going to be another cut.

The thinking that arts and culture organisations are having to do right now is around the question 'How might we manage with less Arts Council England money?' not 'What could we do with more?' It gives me no pleasure at all to say that and, personally, I am deeply worried about the long-term implications on the arts and culture sector. The comments from Danny Boyle et al. on this subject that you mentioned have, as you will have noticed, developed into a full-blown public spat between Maria Miller and (mostly) Nick Hytner and Danny Boyle. It's anyone's guess whether that will result in the government thinking twice about investment in the arts and culture or simply becoming more entrenched in their views.

In the meantime, I am working with Graham on your application to Catalyst 3. This – like the other programmes – will be competitive. We anticipate that there will be eight to twelve grants in London and so far we are aware of over forty expressions of interest at this early stage. Nevertheless, I would dearly love Out of Joint to be one of the recipients and I will do my best to help Graham create the best possible application.

Wishing you all the best as ever.

So it was grim news. Of course, everybody, led by Nick Hytner and Danny Boyle, had to make it clear to the Conservative-led Coalition how damaging the cuts had been. Ed Vaizey, Minister for Culture, was later to echo Maria Miller and claim that this outcry was 'scaremongering' and the theatre was in a rude state of health. Incensed by this wilful wrong-headedness, the playwright Fin Kennedy assembled a 22,000-word report, catchily titled *In Battalions*, which detailed the effect of the cuts on companies across the country. As this journal explains, Out of Joint were compelled to take more conservative programming decisions, but we had been able to sustain our vital research and development work by obtaining funds elsewhere. Not only the National Theare Studio but also the RSC, the Bristol Old Vic, the National Theatre of Wales, the University of Hertfordshire and Bridgend College all gave us help. And as I have already written, 2012/13 was the first year in nineteen years in which Out of Joint produced no new play. At the time of writing, Ed Vaizey continues to dismiss any feelings of alarm and

to date has declined to accept a meeting at which these feelings—
and his no doubt lucid counter-arguments—could be expressed
face to face.

The Arts Council had become increasingly enthusiastic about
assessments and feedback. We normally had an annual review
meeting with them, but they had pressed for further feedback, so I
resolved to send them a complete report on the tour of *Our Country's
Good*.

END-OF-TERM REPORT: OUR COUNTRY'S GOOD

Our Country's Good concluded its twelve-week pre-London
tour on 24th November and this report covers the
rehearsal and tour of the production. The London aspect
of the operation begins on 30th January and runs at the St
James Theatre until 9th March [the run was later
extended]. The first comment to make is that for better or
for worse Out of Joint were pushed into programming
this revival as a direct response to the Arts Council's
pressure to reduce our 'subsidy per seat' ratio. There are
two tried and trusted ways in which a theatre organisation
can increase its audience: by casting Judi Dench (she
wasn't available and she wouldn't tour for twelve weeks)
or by programming a classic. We took the latter course
and *Our Country's Good* in 2012 follows *Top Girls* in 2011.
There is unquestionably a market for *Our Country's Good*,
which continues to be on the exam syllabus. The upside is
that the production has been a very pleasurable
experience both for me and for the actors; however, the
downside is that this is the first year in Out of Joint's
nineteen-year existence in which we will not have
produced a new play. This is, of course, understood by
both ourselves and the Arts Council to be a central part of
Out of Joint's remit and artistic policy.

The rehearsal period was characterised by the unusual step of permitting access to members of the public at a charge of £5 per session. This step proved enormously popular with the public, and all the sessions were sold out in three days. Open rehearsals raised £825 in revenue. It was, however, not popular with the actors, who perhaps understandably felt it inhibited the rehearsal process and took up time which could have been more profitably employed. Their reports are enclosed with two caveats: I certainly wasn't aware of the strength of their resistance at the time, nor do I feel it is entirely just. Certainly the presence of visitors didn't in any way detract from the time devoted to rehearsal. Nonetheless, I heed their resistance, and were we to open our rehearsals again I would certainly be more circumspect and cautious in my approach.

I have trawled the 1,532 assessment forms we have garnered in order to find something negative to lay before you for the sake of balance. One schoolteacher who had taught the play for some years as an English teacher compared the production unfavourably to a school production six years previously. Further investigation revealed that he had subsequently married the drama teacher. There was also a schoolgirl from Cheltenham who thought it was 'too much like a history lesson' and didn't return for the second half, thus missing the bus back to the school and earning herself a prolonged period of detention. But otherwise, the responses (two-thirds of the assessment forms appear to be from students) vary from the enthusiastic to the ecstatic. I have yet to hear from you about the response of your colleagues in Birmingham [I never did], but certainly the responses so far both from the critics and the audience have been that it is Great Art Indeed.

In the course of the tour I conducted a number of workshops, namely at Stonyhurst College, Berkhamsted School, St Bernard's Slough and Pocklington College, and for several schools who attended the Nuffield Theatre in Southampton; below is a selection of responses.

> The students had a wonderful time and it was a real pleasure and privilege for us to have met you.
>
> *Education Officer, West Yorkshire Playhouse*

> It was an absolute honour to work with Max, and to get an insight into his teaching and how he makes you deliver every line with a different emotion. The performance we went to see of *Our Country's Good* was absolutely brilliant, capturing so many different emotions in one small play. Amazing!
>
> *Student, Berkhamsted School*

> I think the workshop was really useful in terms of understanding the background to the characters. Using the cards to denote status was a really good idea, and improved my understanding of the status of the characters and how to portray that. I thought giving each line an intention was a really useful exercise, and was helpful in terms of describing in an essay how an actor would act something. However, I think the workshop could have been divided up better as we only had half an hour on the actual script of the play out of a two-hour workshop. I really enjoyed watching the performance, and the actors use of the techniques we had been shown in the workshop was clear, which was interesting to see.
>
> *Student, Berkhamsted School*

> Our workshop on *Our Country's Good* was a very interactive, educating and entertaining experience.

Max Stafford-Clark is a very thought-provoking man full of brilliant ideas and techniques and it was a pleasure to bear witness to his teaching.

Student, Berkhamsted School

The workshop with Max Stafford-Clark was also very interesting as we were able to concentrate on the hierarchy and status of people by how they acted and responded to others and how they spoke. It was also helpful to see Max's style of working through a script because he cut down each line and really analysed what it was they were saying and how they said it. Both the production and workshop were really inspiring and have made me appreciate the play so much more!

Student, Berkhamsted School

All exercises were really helpful and really enjoyable to take part in.

Student, Stonyhurst College

Learnt useful information from Max about the play and its origin, which is great towards my studies. Being more involved would have been great, even though it was very interesting watching him work with the few actors, it would have been good if more of us could have been involved.

Student, Stonyhurst College

I wanted to see a typical rehearsal with Max and understand actioning and see it put to use – it was very successful.

Student, St Bernard's, Slough

For those at the back of the class, I should remind you what the Berkhamsted student is talking about:

> [GUIDES] I have detailed the technique of actioning in both *Letters to George* and *Taking Stock*, but [TEACHES] briefly, it is the notion of selecting a transitive verb to indicate each change of thought [INTRIGUES] and then the next stage is actually verbalising the verb before the line. So this last sentence I have written, I have dissected as 'guides', 'teaches', 'intrigues'. Hopefully the whole sentence comes within the overall objective of 'teaches', or perhaps more ambitiously, bearing in mind that I have now made you read about the workings of the Arts Council for more than one hundred and fifty pages, 'fascinates'.

I also sent Frank feedback from some of the actors, many of whom focused on our opening rehearsals to paying punters. John Hollingworth, who played Governor Phillip and Wisehammer, a born leader and alumnus of my alma mater, Trinity College Dublin, had made the most impassioned stand:

> I'll be brief and honest. It's a strange position to be put in, being asked to critique your employer, when every actor needs a company that will give them work.

> That Out of Joint tours so much is commendable. Thirteen weeks away from home felt one week too long for me.

> What made the job a no-brainer, apart from the chance to play two such different characters, was of course Max. However, the early weeks of rehearsal were infuriating because of the observers. Firstly, to not have been consulted *at all* before being subjected to them was deeply offensive. I would definitely have thought twice about not taking the job if I'd known beforehand. Once we're in the room we've no choice but to be pliant animals—to be otherwise retards the early cohesion of a company and

knocks one's relationship with a company off-kilter. That's exactly what the observers did: disrupted the valuable coming-together of a company and distanced everybody from Out of Joint. We had no free space, the observers butting in and chatting upstairs in the green room, outside on the smoking benches and over the road in the café. It was Bolton before many of us got to know each other.

Having not worked for Out of Joint before I didn't ask the questions of Max about actioning and process that I would have liked to, because suddenly we were being presented to observers as professionals. The actions I assigned to and negotiated for my characters were often done more out of classroom pleasantries than meaningful work. That's the sticking point. We work so fucking hard for so long and so little that to be robbed the dignity of doing it seriously and for each other and the play rather than for a bunch of interested amateurs rankles deeply indeed. The courtesies and pleasantries extended to them by Max only served to embolden them and make them think that their opinion actually counted. They should have kept their mouths shut.

I said I'd be brief and I've not been, but this stuff matters. I hope you can hold the observers up to the Arts Council as an example of what you as a company have had to sacrifice in order to comply with their request to diversify revenue streams and cope with their punitive cuts. Given that an increase in funding seems impossible in these dark austerity days, if you have to raise funds through observing I'd do it like this. Give the actors the first week entirely alone. Charge the observers three times as much and only have them in the second week for no more than three days, and the third week for no more than two. Ticket the second and third runthroughs where their presence could be a useful indicator of what's to come.

I hope this book serves to fulfil the desire John outlines in his final paragraph.

3rd December 2012

Dear Frank,

Thank you so much for your email which arrived on Friday evening, so I haven't absorbed it sufficiently to respond in detail although I very much appreciate the warmth of your response to *Our Country's Good*. Graham and I anticipated that it would be unlikely that there would be any further funding available for our education work, so we will effect Plan B, in which he and I will each contribute £500 to bolster our current education programme. This will mean we will be able to cap the fee for all workshops to £100 for the remainder of the financial year, and we will run a training day for workshop leaders (probably some time in February). I have noted with interest the current debate on arts funding: it will do no harm, and it may even do some good.

We have 1,500 assessment forms in the office with a further sackful yet to arrive from Leeds. I should explain that we encountered considerable local difficulty in distributing the assessment forms: for example, at the Birmingham Old Rep there are no front-of-house staff called until the half [i.e. thirty-five minutes before curtain up], and this of course coincides with a particularly busy time for our stage-management team which made communication particularly difficult. Consequently no forms were distributed and at the get-out a whole stack of blank forms was discovered at the back of the auditorium. Watford had their own forms and were consequently reluctant to distribute yet another. Their form focused on the price of drinks and the comfort of the seats and had no questions that addressed the performance. Jon Bradfield has carefully logged and annotated the responses while I have read in detail every tenth form. Of the 150 I read, 148 were extremely positive, and two were negative: one person finding the play tedious and the other finding fault with the acting. The respondees had an older demographic than I had anticipated: there were many students, but the more detailed responses tended to come from punters in the 50+ age range.

I had initially imagined that your enthusiasm for assessment forms was to give feedback to you. It wasn't until your conversation with Panda that I realised the assessment information was for us. Of course, we will continue to garner assessments when we next do a production (this time next year), but I must say that I find it a singularly pointless exercise. It might perhaps be more helpful with a new or unknown play, but it does seem a prolonged and labour-intensive way of finding out what was in any case quite obvious: that the vast majority of the audience enjoyed the play very much. It is after all a well-known and much-loved classic. As I have detailed already, there was a very small minority who found *Top Girls* a baffling and frustrating experience, but no such resistance was encountered here. Trawling back through the last twenty years I have enclosed a table of comparative attendance figures. It compares figures for both *Our Country's Good* and *Top Girls* to 'threatening' and 'non-threatening' productions both in the early years of Out of Joint's existence (1998/99) and a mid-period (around 2005). I'm not absolutely clear what conclusions can be drawn from this, but it does suggest that the public's tolerance and appetite for 'threatening' work has waned. In retrospect, the figures for *Drummers* (a flawed play by a completely unknown, and flawed, house burglar) seem astonishingly high. We would certainly not get such a positive response today. I am trying my best to be positive, but I do find the insistence on 'assessments' to be a singularly pointless exercise. Why don't we just tell you how we're doing? We always know, I promise.

James Brining seems inclined towards *Ciphers*, although he is still planning his first year. News from New York drags on without seeming to get any closer to a decision.

Production	>500	400–500	300–400	200–300	100–200	0–100
Blue Heart (1997) Non-threatening			3	4		
Drummers (1999) Threatening					5	
The Permanent Way (2003) Non-threatening	3	1	5		1	
Talking to Terrorists (2005) Threatening			1	3	5	1
Bang Bang Bang (2011) Threatening					4	2
Tops Girls (2011) Non-threatening		3	1	4	1	
Our Country's Good (2012) Non-threatening			2	6	1	

On Monday 3rd December, our board member and benefactor, Karl Sydow, hosted a lunch for the London theatre critics at the Garrick Club. It was a revival of a practice I had started at the Royal Court; the annual lunch permitted both sets of antagonists to emerge from the trenches and fraternise. I used the occasion to brief the critics on the reasons for Out of Joint's rather conservative programming decisions and to launch the London run of *Our Country's Good* at the St James. Bookings were good, and the season had now been extended by two weeks until 23rd March 2013. Michael Coveney wrote an extensive and sympathetic blog and Richard Brooks wrote of our dilemma in his *Sunday Times* column after Christmas.

On 7th December a final word came back that no extra funding for education work would be available. At the same time an application under the Freedom of Information Act revealed the cost of the absurd brochure 'Achieving Great Art for Everyone'...

10th December 2012

Dear Frank,

I was sad to learn finally that there is no funding available to support our education programme... particularly as 'Achieving Great Art for Everyone' proclaims that 'we will champion high-quality opportunities for young people to enjoy the arts in and out of school'. Several phone calls to the Arts Council enquiring as to the cost of 'Achieving Great Art for Everyone' had been unsuccessful, but an application under the Freedom of Information Act revealed last week that the costs of the design, printing and distribution of the pamphlet were £31,307. The same application also told me that the Arts Council holds reserves of £141,730,000. You will understand that my disappointment turned to rage and disgust at this information and at the hypocrisy of the Arts Council. I understand that you have no authority or mandate to authorise my request, but to whom then should my concerns be more properly addressed? I also had a response from Maria Miller last week, who wrote that she was 'unable to meet because of excessive diary commitments', and suggested I should 'address my concerns to the Arts Council'. Yes, but to whom? Please let me know and I will submit a final application. [He never did.]

On Thursday Allan Buchman phoned to tell me that he no longer had the funds to schedule *Dr Johnson* at the Culture Project in the spring. It was not a play he felt came within the remit of the Culture Project. In truth he has never been enthusiastic about it. I countered that my commitment to *The Seagull* was dependent on both projects going ahead, and I could not justify ten weeks away from Out of Joint if the company had no work represented in his proposed season. I withdrew my commitment to *The Seagull*. It was all off. Graham and I then examined the existing dates we had in London at Dr Johnson's House, in Southampton and in Dublin. Without the production costs being shared with New York, the unacceptable cost would be about £11,800, and because houses would be small the impact on our 'subsidy per seat' ratio would not be significant. Nonetheless, I felt disappointed: my enthusiasm for the whole project had sprung from the opportunity to make Out of Joint's work more widely known. However, on Friday Allan Buchman called back to say it was all on again. He had been able to shift the dates of a fundraising event, which apparently would ease his cash-flow situation. So it's on, but I anticipate several more vagaries before the programme becomes a reality.

Finally, I am juggling dates for *Ciphers* next autumn. Blanche McIntyre has been offered another directing job at the Almeida which, were she to accept it, would make her unavailable in September. Madani Younis at the Bush can only offer the possibility of September otherwise it would have to be after Christmas. James Brining at the West Yorkshire Playhouse cannot take it before October if he takes it at all, and Ed Hall at Hampstead hasn't responded yet but has a planning meeting in the middle of this week. Greg Doran also has a planning meeting in the middle of December, at which *Pitcairn* will be discussed. I have arranged pre-Christmas meetings with Robin Soans (Gareth Thomas) and Rebecca Lenkiewicz (*Witches*) at which they will both deliver their initial drafts. Stella Feehily is giving a delivery draft of *This May Hurt A Bit* to the National Theatre at the end of January.

At this point everything except the London run of *Our Country's Good* was shifting and uncertain. *Ciphers* couldn't be pinned down, and there was no tangible commitment from any of our prospective co-producers for the plays in development. The critics had been set the task following the lunch at the Garrick Club of programming the next two years for Out of Joint. There were prizes. Their ideas were expensive and hugely impractical; Michael Billington and Jane Edwardes proposed the politically incorrect but historically accurate and titillating notion of topless Tahitian maidens to sell Richard Bean's *Pitcairn*, but Michael Coveney finally won the prize with a deft union between Gareth Thomas and the NHS. However, before Christmas all these projects looked sadly distant and beyond our reach. Even *Ciphers* looked less than certain. I found the precariousness of the future more debilitating than anything and was desperate to find some firm ground. The programme in New York was also nebulous.

17th December 2012

Dear Frank,

A Dish of Tea with Dr Johnson in New York has finally fallen through. Karl Sydow was unable to come to an investment agreement with Allan Buchman and without that guarantee, Allan withdrew. *The Seagull* goes ahead, and I finally agreed to do it, not least because there is little opportunity of directing here until late 2013 at the earliest.

Discussions about *Ciphers* continue and Graham has meetings next week with Rachel Tyson from the Bush and James Brining from the West Yorkshire Playhouse. The plan would be to open in Leeds in October and tour for six weeks before a run at the Bush starting in January. Ed Hall at Hampstead felt that Dawn King would not be served well by a production in his downstairs studio space, but that the play was not appropriate for Hampstead's main stage. He has some justification. Despite the praise she has garnered, this will mark Dawn King's graduation from the unsubsidised fringe (the Finborough) to the subsidised sector. The Theatre Upstairs, the Bush or Soho Theatre would all be appropriate venues and presumably it will tour to theatres of similar size, which brings me to 'subsidy per seat'. I have no doubt that the route we have chosen is best for Dawn King and for Blanche McIntyre, but is it a sensible course for Out of Joint? With the National Theatre of Wales not able to co-produce until 2014/15, *Ciphers* will be Out of Joint's sole production in the financial year 2013/14, and audiences will necessarily be small. I seek your reassurance that Out of Joint won't be punished for that at the next round of funding awards.

On Saturday I spent the day in Salisbury on a ten-hour visit working with six writers in the development programme we have instigated with the Salisbury Playhouse, who do not have the funds for a literary manager. I believe in education. I believe in access. I have always maintained that it is of great importance to any new-writing organisation 'to keep the back door unlocked' and encourage approaches from writers who are not in the circle of 'professional' writers we turn to for commissions. The day went well; the writers were happy and grateful, and at least two of them showed some promise. So why do I still feel some lingering resentment and bile towards the Arts Council? Perhaps because I know that the real reason for the visit is the couple of hundred quid that Out of Joint will make to prove to you that we are 'diversifying our streams of income' – or is it that I feel it would be a better use of my time and Out of Joint's resources if I were actually directing a play?

You may have noticed an article by Charlotte Higgins in the *Guardian* last week lamenting the paucity of opportunity for women writers and for actresses. It is worth pointing out that 15 of the 34 plays Out of Joint have produced, or 44%, are by women, and that 100% of our output in 2011, 2012 and 2013 will have been authored by women.

Finally, on a personal note, I am delighted to tell you that I have been given the Critics' Circle Centenary Award for services to the arts in drama. I am delighted and flattered. This news is confidential until it has been announced by the Critics' Circle, but you are a Friend so I can tell you everything.

With unusual swiftness, Frank replied the very same day.

Dear Max,

I was just finishing off my response to Friday's letter when this email arrived.

It is, of course, a shame that *Ciphers* will be Out of Joint's sole production in the financial year 2013/14 [I was wrong: *This May Hurt A Bit* would have four of its ten touring weeks in 2013/14] – although this is tempered by the anticipation of seeing what sounds like an excellent piece. Although it may sometimes feel like it, I can assure you we do not set out to 'punish' anyone. However, beyond that, I'm afraid I cannot say much about how the next funding round will proceed – for the simple reason that we don't know. We don't know when it will happen or what the criteria will be; nor do we know what our likely budget will be, although I think it is reasonable – and, indeed, deeply worrying – to assume that we will have even less budget than now.

I'm sorry you feel rage and disgust about the cost of publishing 'Great Art for Everyone' and the level of Arts Council reserves. £142m in reserves may sound large but, of course, size is relative. Compared with our turnover in 2011/12 of £613m, this level is similar to other organisations and indeed is significantly less than, for example, Out of Joint's. Furthermore, if you look closely at the Financial Review where you got those figures you will see that the vast majority of those reserves are restricted and that our unrestricted reserves at March 2012 were only £3.2m. In any case, we have to manage our reserves under fairly tight restrictions from the DCMS, which limit manoeuvre. Also, our core business, so to speak, is the distribution of money. Tens of millions of pounds pass through our accounts most months to thousands of organisation and individuals. Consequently, the cash flow that has to be managed is complex. This is most acute with our Lottery money – not least because the percentage of our turnover that is Lottery has been inexorably rising over the last few years and is expected to hit 50% in the next few years. We have to make grant commitments with Lottery money sometimes years ahead – for example, Catalyst and Capital – without necessarily knowing that we will receive those funds. Lottery income is volatile and unpredictable – receipts rose at the start of the recession, for example, but have been falling through most of this year. The setting of our reserves level is a constant balance between the need to safely cover commitments, manage risks, DCMS and National Audit Office requirements and the desire to make funds available. Unrestricted reserves of £3.2m as a fund to maintain liquidity (cash flow), to cover unforeseen short-term cash requirements and to cover planned future expenditure on such a level of turnover, is, I would suggest, on the low side.

There is a need to have some understanding of what the Arts Council does, or tries to do and what its priorities are. This makes a document like 'Achieving Great Art for Everyone' absolutely essential. Whilst many people access it online (it is the second most read document in the Advice and Guidance section on our website), not everyone likes or is willing to do this; hence the print run.

I think, given the sheer range and number of people who need or would like to read it, £31,307 is remarkably good value for money.

I understand your disappointment that there is not currently a mechanism by which you can ask for £1,000 towards your education work – that there is not, as you put it, someone who can authorise your request. However, I believe that a moment's reflection would make it clear why this is so. If such a mechanism did exist, then why shouldn't the other 700-odd NPOs request and receive £1,000? What about the non-NPO arts organisations, Major Partner Museums, Museum Development Providers, Music Education Hubs and so on? Where would it end and indeed why should it be £1,000 as opposed to some other figure?

One of the points of a public-money funding system organisation is that it is *not* a patronage system or a kind of Dragon's Den, where money is given out based on individual requests and pleadings. It means that, as far as possible, there are guidelines and criteria in how the money is distributed. In order for that to happen, there have to be funding programmes, each with its own eligibility, criteria and assessment processes in place. That begs the question, how do you decide on and design the programmes, criteria, etc.? In our case, our funding programmes are designed around and against a strategic framework – something which attempts to set out what's important for the next ten years for the arts and cultural sector. This brings us back to 'Achieving Great Art for Everyone'. This is that ten-year framework – a series of goals that are considered important, around which funding programmes can be designed to complement or help deliver. As for its contents – you personally may not like them, but I can assure you we didn't impose our thoughts on an unwilling sector. We consulted widely – some would say excessively – on what was important. I don't think anyone would say the document was perfect; but for the five main headline areas for focus (the 'Goals') that – broadly speaking – are: Artistic excellence; Audiences; Talent development for the next generation; Stronger organisations; Children and young people – there was, and remains, broad agreement within the sector.

The document itself isn't perfect – and the panoply of administering funding programmes with their assessments and criteria and monitoring is not sexy and is very often clunky – but it at least tries to be fair and open within a (by and large) agreed framework.

So, again, I am sorry that this upsets you, and I am also sorry that we currently are unable to respond positively to your request. The fact that you and Graham are willing to contribute £500 to bolster the programme is yet another example of both of your deep commitment and which I very much admire and respect.

I am glad that discussions for *Pitcairn* are still ongoing as I thought it was a really strong and powerful piece. Incidentally, I don't know if you know, but Captain Bligh's grave is near here; it's in the graveyard of the converted church that is now home to the Garden Museum next to Lambeth Palace (I was there for a meeting last week). You can see it when you walk round the grounds – weirdly, it's next to a 'secret door' that goes between Lambeth Palace and the church grounds. Please keep me informed of progress on the production as well, of course, on Stella's excellent *This May Hurt A Bit* and *Ciphers*.

I am delighted at the level of response that you are getting with your evaluation, and it is very good that you seem to be getting such high levels of positive responses. I look forward to seeing further collation and analyses of them.

Best wishes as ever and, of course, many congratulations on your award.

If I don't get the chance again, may I take this opportunity to wish you and yours a very happy Christmas.

The only problem with asking the Arts Council a question is that occasionally you get an answer with such a baffling series of acronyms that it takes a week to decipher. However, in this case at least, the overall response was clear: the answer was 'no'. As it has always been 'no', right through the course of this journal.

*

So, after eighteen months of attempting to engage with our 'Relationship Manager', had I got anywhere? Had I achieved anything? No further financial help had been forthcoming for cold spots, for commissions or for education work. But the truth is that for all my bile and my deep-seated sense of grievance against them, the Arts Council are but the agency of a Conservative-led Coalition government in headlong pursuit of economies and with no great understanding of or sympathy for the theatre. In the words of Oscar Wilde, they know 'the price of everything and the value of nothing'. The future seems bleak, as Endwright wrote: 'We are in a completely different financial situation. I think it is reasonable, and indeed deeply worrying, to assume that we will have even less budget than now.' For nearly fifty years I had worked in a theatre supported by the knowledge and belief that good work would be rewarded and supported by the state. In association with our partners at the National Theatre Studio, the RSC, the Bristol Old Vic, the National Theatre of Wales and the University of Hertfordshire, we have spent 2012 developing four cracking plays, as well as lending our support to a fifth already-existing script, Dawn King's *Ciphers*. I have no doubts about the importance, freshness, originality and pertinence of that play or of *Pitcairn*, *This May Hurt A Bit*, *Crouch, Touch, Hold, Engage* or *Rough Music*.

What is in doubt at the time of writing are the funding and co-production partnerships necessary to get these terrific plays on the stage. When I was Artistic Director of the Traverse Theatre, Edinburgh, in the 1960s, my first relationship with a Scottish Arts

Council officer had been with Ronald 'Bingo' Mavor, newly retired from the Indian civil service. It was a time when the *Scottish Daily Express* was still monitoring the number of occasions the word 'bloody' was used in a particular play. 'I won't always approve of what you chaps are doing,' Mavor said candidly, 'and I certainly won't always understand it, but remember I'm always at the end of a phone if you get into trouble.' Those avuncular days are long gone, but I must beware the constant condition of complaint that is perforce my default position with the Arts Council.

Towards the end of my time at the Royal Court I directed a play, *Etta Jenks*, by Marlane Meyer, a screenwriter from California. I liked her very much and we spent several pleasant evenings drinking together. She taught me a lesson. One night in the Groucho Club, or maybe it was the Zanzibar, she asked me in a general way how the Royal Court was doing. I at once embarked on a litany of complaint that embraced the leaks in the roof, the Equity-imposed rise in actors' salaries and, doubtless, the parsimony of the Arts Council. 'Why are you always complaining?' said Marlane. 'You're doing a job you love with people you love and you're funded to do it, now for God's sake shut up.' She was right. I've had nearly fifty wonderful years working on plays and with people that I love; it's just sad to think that it may be coming to an end. Certainly it became too much for my valued colleague and companion of forty years, Graham Cowley, who told me last week that he intended to retire in May 2013 when he had reached his sixty-fifth birthday. The Catalyst 3, Tier 4 funding consortium was the straw that broke the camel's back; the Arts Council wish us to apply for funding which explicitly cannot be used for any artistic purpose but must be devoted to training schemes aimed at making us efficient fundraisers. 'If that's the way forward,' he said, 'I just don't think I have the appetite for it any more.'

While writing the last dozen pages I have been reading Michael Blakemore's excellent memoir, *Arguments with England*. He is wise enough to conclude his book with the triumphant arrival of *A Day in the Death of Joe Egg* in the West End, and his appointment as Associate Director of the National Theatre. Alas, no such exhilarating ending is available to me; *Our Country's Good* did well in its run at the St James Theatre, is scheduled for revival next year to go to Minneapolis and Toronto. That'll be fun, but the recession and the hysterical rush to austerity is with us still. Things will get better, because it's the theatre and they always do, but chillingly not just yet: the plague has not completely run its course.

Epilogue

As a matter of politeness I thought I had better send a copy of the finished manuscript to Frank Endwright. I did so on 28th May. There was a silence for a couple of weeks before Frank replied, 'We are still looking at it.' I responded that I had not submitted the manuscript to Arts Council England for vetting and approval, but rather had sent it to him as a friend and unwitting participant for his perusal and comment. Again there was a pause of several weeks before Frank's superior at the Arts Council, George Darling, responded that Frank 'felt he had a duty' to share the manuscript widely within the Arts Council. George went on to write, 'We are within our rights to refuse consent to publish, and while we're not intending to do so' requested anonymity for our Relationship Manager. So, dear reader, you may peruse lists of Arts Council personnel in vain; there is no Frank Endwright. I realise the 'nom de plume' expresses a reckless optimism about our dialogue with the Arts Council, but it has a pleasant Restoration resonance that I like— and George Darling is, of course, the name of Wendy's dad in *Peter Pan*. In a subsequent email George warned me that if ACE received 'any enquiries from the media we may wish to represent another view and that may include information you are not currently intending to publish'. I replied that I was unclear what he intended by this veiled threat, but I was happy for him to do so and that I would welcome details of 'inaccuracies' that George had mentioned earlier. He responded that he had no time to catalogue such details and we left it at that... The Relationship continues.

Appendix 1

Out of Joint was not the only company to be devastated by the cuts. Our colleagues at the Almeida and at Shared Experience were similarly blighted, and in Shared Experience's case, their entire Arts Council grant withdrawn. Polly Teale, one of the Artistic Directors of Shared Experience, recounts her outrage and shock:

> My company, Shared Experience, has pioneered a distinctive performance style, bringing new plays and classics to life in bold, imaginative ways. The company has created a number of groundbreaking productions that have influenced generations of theatre-makers. Despite huge popularity borne out by high attendance figures and frequent critical success the company's current production may be the last Shared Experience show funded by the Arts Council.

> Like hundreds of others I awoke early on the 30th of March last year as I awaited the phone call with news of the Arts Council's funding decision. We had been celebrating the night before. Shared Experience had just become the resident company at Oxford Playhouse and opened our latest production *Brontë* to a fantastic response from a packed house. The move to Oxford Playhouse was designed to save the company £90,000 a year. A move which the Arts Council had encouraged and which had taken a huge amount of work and careful planning. After the opening night, we had a party to launch this exciting new partnership. Early the next morning it was with utter disbelief that I heard the voice on the other end of the line tell me that we had lost our entire Arts Council grant. I could not believe my ears and had to ask three times in order for the words to sink in. A year later I am still reeling.

Shared Experience is run by two women, myself and
Nancy Meckler. Despite some startling exceptions it
remains the case that less than one in four theatre
directors are female, although lists of aspiring young
theatre directors are dominated by women. As we all
know, the profession continues to employ far more men
both on and off stage. This is partly because it has ever
been thus. The canon of plays favours men over women.
Reflecting the times in which they were written, in
many great plays women are wives, mothers, lovers,
maids, but rarely the centre of the story.

So why you would wonder has the Arts Council
chosen to completely sever all funding to a successful
company run by women that has promoted the work
of female writers, directors, designers, producers and
most visibly, actors? We have created a canon of
acclaimed plays that provide meaty female parts that
explore women's experience in all its complexity,
placing woman centre-stage.

The Arts Council funding criteria has changed
significantly in recent months. The emphasis shifting
away from the artist and the depth and quality of the
work to 'provision', with the focus on audience
statistics and 'value for money', on how many people
see a production versus what it costs to make. Whilst I
completely understand and recognise the importance
of making ourselves as accessible and affordable as
possible, it fails to take account of the unique nature
of our work and the conditions needed in order to
achieve its depth, psychological complexity and
ambition, the very things that make it worth funding.

Michael Attenborough, then Artistic Director of the Almeida, also recorded his shock:

> Along with the news of our cut, we were sent by ACE a report on our work describing us as 'an exemplary organisation, performing to the highest possible artistic standards'; but we had made the big mistake of accumulating a surplus of £2.7m, as reserves for future capital and revenue needs. So when ACE were desperately looking round for any spare cash, we were clearly vulnerable. Aside from being punished for success, my main grievance was that they were not more open at the point of announcement about their view of us as an artistic organisation. The fallout from the cut was not only financial, it was combatting any possible resultant sense of stigma amongst our other key stakeholders and supporters. I think ACE have a responsibility to manage such situations with more intelligence and sophistication, in order to limit as much collateral damage as possible as a result of their actions, in the face of which we are, of course, defenceless.

Following this news, Nancy Meckler was so downcast and dispirited that she understandably stood down from Shared Experience, leaving Polly Teale to fight for project grants in order to continue.[1] Michael Attenborough, too, stepped away from the Almeida.

---

1. Out of Joint does not entirely reflect the imbalanced demographic Polly Teale points to. As I outlined to the Arts Council, fifteen of the thirty-four productions we have produced, or 44%, have been written by women, and from 2011 to 2013 Out of Joint's entire output was by women playwrights. However, our figures are by no means typical.

Appendix 2

Out of Joint Budget for 2012/13

Budget for 2012/2013, July 2013 Version	Original Budget	Year-end Projection	Year-end Variance
Summary			
INCOME			
Tour fees/box office – England	141,000	141,000	–
Box office – London	388,965	388,965	–
Co-production contributions	69,930	69,930	–
Tour fees – abroad	–	–	–
British Council	–	–	–
Arts Council	523,328	423,986	-99,342
Arts Council G4A replacement	25,475	–	-25,475
Education	3,550	3,550	–
Fundraising income	20,000	20,000	–
Sponsorship	–	–	–
Bank interest	2,000	2,000	–
Matured commissions	10,000	10,000	–
Royalties	250	250	–
Net playtext income	2,650	2,650	–
Other net trading income	5,600	5,600	–
Total Income	**1,192,748**	**1,067,931**	**-124,817**
EXPENDITURE			
Production costs – England	300,464	300,464	–
Production costs – London	326,174	326,174	–
Production costs – abroad	–	–	–
Theatre writing	58,984	58,984	–
Education	3,090	3,090	–
Staff salaries and fees	301,311	283,066	-18,244
Administration	54,100	43,100	-11,000
Overheads	53,053	53,053	–
Total Expenditure	**1,097,175**	**1,067,931**	**-29,244**
Net surplus (deficit)	**95,573**	**0**	**-95,573**
SURPLUS brought forward	354,953	354,953	–
SURPLUS carried forward	450,526	354,953	-95,573

Summary of All Productions

	Our Country's Good								All productions	
	PRE-PRODUCTION		LONDON		TOUR		TOTALS		TOTALS	
	BUDGET	ESTIMATED ACTUAL	BUDGET	ESTIMATED ACTUAL	BUDGET	ESTIMATED ACTUAL	BUDGET	ESTIMATED ACTUAL	BUDGET	ESTIMATED ACTUAL
Wages	36,640	36,640	102,392	102,392	74,808	74,808	213,839	213,839	213,839	213,839
Fees/Royalties	23,000	23,000	21,500	21,500	–	–	44,500	44,500	44,500	44,500
Physical costs	40,200	40,200	7,250	7,250	6,000	6,000	53,450	53,450	53,450	53,450
Touring costs	–	–	9,500	9,500	78,140	78,140	87,640	87,640	87,640	87,640
Publicity/Marketing	2,000	2,000	50,000	50,000	26,400	26,400	78,400	78,400	78,400	78,400
Theatre writing	–	–	–	–	840	840	840	840	840	840
Education	–	–	21,000	21,000	–	–	21,000	21,000	21,000	21,000
Theatre costs	–	–	100,000	100,000	–	–	100,000	100,000		
Admin	–	–	20,000	20,000	4,400	4,400	24,400	24,400	24,400	24,400
	101,840	101,840	331,642	331,642	190,588	190,588	624,069	624,069	624,069	624,069
Contingencies	3,055	3,055	15,532	15,532	5,821	5,821	24,409	24,409	24,409	24,409
TOTAL COST	104,895	104,895	347,174	347,174	196,409	196,409	648,478	648,478	648,478	648,478
Fees	–	–	–	–	141,000	141,000	141,000	141,000		
Box office	–	–	388,965	388,965	–	–	388,965	388,965	388,965	388,965
Co-production	69,930	69,930	–	–	–	–	69,930	69,930	69,930	69,930
Public sector	–	–	–	–	–	–	–	–	–	–
Sponsorship	–	–	–	–	–	–	–	–	–	–
Education	–	–	–	–	1,050	1,050	1,050	1,050	1,050	1,050
Other income	300,464	300,464	–	–	–	–	–	–	–	–
TOTAL INCOME	69,930	69,930	388,965	388,965	142,050	142,050	600,945	600,945	600,945	600,945
Surplus/(Deficit)	-34,965	-34,965	41,791	41,791	-54,359	-54,359	-47,533	-47,533	-47,533	-47,533

Appendix 3

Recession has made British audiences more conservative, says playwright (by Matt Trueman, 9th February 2012)

Simon Stephens claims people's theatre tastes have shifted over the past three years 'towards the commercial and the accessible'.

British theatre audiences have become more conservative since the recession, the Olivier Award-winning playwright Simon Stephens has claimed.

In an interview with the website Theatrevoice, Stephens said: 'I think people's taste for theatre, in the past three years, has shifted more towards the commercial and the accessible.'

Claiming to find the change in audience behaviour 'curious and troubling', the playwright, whose recent plays include *Wastwater* and *Punk Rock*, argued that it relates directly to the current economic climate.

'The years, from say 1996 to 2006, were years of comparative affluence, safety, comfort, and you look at the theatre that was being made; it was theatre that was searching, savage, violent, sexually dark, psychologically dark. So at a time of affluence, audiences seem drawn to an artform that was kind of difficult.'

'The defining plays of the end of the '90s were, say, *Blasted* and *Shopping and Fucking*. The defining plays of the last three years are possibly *Jerusalem*, *Enron* and *One Man, Two Guvnors*,' he continued. 'The fundamental actions of [all three plays], it strikes me, is to entertain, to uplift, to inspire, to tickle.'

The commercial sector has regularly defied the recession since it began, with the Society of London Theatre announcing record-breaking West

End revenue for the past nine years. However, the number of attendees have dipped each year since 2009.

By contrast, Stephens admitted that ticket sales for *The Trial of Ubu*, his latest play currently playing at the Hampstead Theatre, have been 'really poor', and suggested a number of possible factors, including mixed reviews and recent cold weather. At last Saturday evening's performance, which coincided with snowfall, Stephens estimated that 54 people were in the 277-seat auditorium.

Stephens stressed the importance of experimental theatre, despite it being 'difficult to sell'. He continued: 'It's urgent that the state-subsidised theatres continue to stage work that is not going to find an audience,' he said, before joking that they 'should be playing to 30%, because that's what state subsidy is for'.

In *ArtsProfessional* magazine's 2010 survey, in which a fifth of respondents self-identified as leaders of an arts organisation, 41% said they would programme more 'popular' work as a result of the recession, while 37% anticipated reducing the amount of 'challenging' work they commissioned.

Edward Hall, Artistic Director of Hampstead Theatre, said: '*The Trial of Ubu* is not a sell-out, but continues to provoke and delight those who see it – and is indicative of the form-breaking work that any theatre that holds the impulse of new writing at its centre should aspire to.'

Regional theatres must take risks too – so why isn't the Arts Council helping? (by Max Stafford-Clark, 27th February 2012)

There's an easy way to please the Arts Council: sell as many tickets as you can. That isn't the same as challenging audiences.

Theatre isn't rocket science. Audiences want what they always wanted – comedy, sex, romance, frocks, satire and a soupçon of political provocation. When Out of Joint, the theatre company I run, has provided those things, our audience figures have exceeded expectations. But when we do more difficult work (such as our recent shows *Talking to Terrorists*, *The Big Fellah* and *Bang Bang Bang*) regional audiences have been disappointing, especially before the imprimatur of London reviews.

This work may appeal to fewer people, but that does not make it less important, less special or less pertinent to people's lives. We know this from our audiences. Our post-show discussions with audiences for Stella Feehily's *Bang Bang Bang*, which focuses on a humanitarian worker in the Congo, were the most rewarding, engaging and intelligent we've experienced. The richness of experience, the surprise of the new, is every bit as important as reaching the widest possible audience.

Arts Council England was founded to disseminate and champion such work. Mark Ravenhill was right to say last week that the nature of subsidy appears to be changing, and is far more tied to audience sizes. In common with other theatre companies and arts organisations, Out of Joint has received a damaging cut. We have been assured by the Arts Council that the excellence of our work is not in question, but that the subsidy per seat is too high.

In 2010/11, the year on which this assessment was made, we played to 22,888 people. Ironically, in the year about to end, we estimate this figure will be in excess of 52,250 people. Caution and conservative programming have certainly played a part in doubling this figure. We are currently touring Caryl Churchill's 1982 play *Top Girls* to large audiences. Our next production will also be a revival, Timberlake Wertenbaker's *Our Country's Good*. Both are brilliant plays, and we're thrilled to introduce them to a new generation. But it will be the first time in nineteen years that we have gone a year without producing a new play.

This is a national issue. In London there will always be some sort of platform for less commercial work. As a touring company, we exist to take productions to other parts of the country. In places where there is perhaps just one theatre, it only takes that venue to play cautious for financial reasons for their audience to be excluded from anything but mainstream work. The message seems to be: get conservative, or perish.

Appendix 4

The report by Naomi Jones on the Verbatim Theatre Workshop at Oxford Playhouse in August 2012.

Having worked on a number of verbatim theatre projects, both during my time as Asistant Director at Out of Joint and as a freelance director, I have a keen interest in the form. I was therefore delighted to be asked by Out of Joint to lead a week's workshop investigating the specific methodology of verbatim theatre, together with other rehearsal techniques used by Max Stafford-Clark, in a project supported by Oxford Playhouse.

Theme

The week's research took the very broad title of 'town and gown' as its basis, but looked more specifically at the tradition of 'trashing' and other traditions associated with the finals exam season at Oxford University. In the process of researching this topic we spoke to two students, a Senior Lecturer in History at Keble College and a Clerk to the Proctors' office. We also interviewed stallholders at the famous covered market, homeless people and very colourful ex-student turned town guide.

Participants

The group of ten participants ranged dramatically in age and experience. The youngest member of the group was seventeen and had never done drama before, there was a student who was in the process of preparing his application to write a Phd on verbatim theatre, as well as a gentlemen of sixty who upon retirement had decided to become a playwright. Whilst I was not expecting such diversity (the workshop having been advertised as part of Oxford Playhouse's Summer Holiday season), it actually proved to be a great asset to project. It meant that discussions about the logistics, ethics and application of the verbatim theatre form were wide-ranging and in depth and participants were keen to follow their own interests and leads in the research tasks.

Schedule

As several members of the group were interested in the rehearsal techniques of Out of Joint, it was important to work towards a performance at the end of the week, which enabled the participants to work with actioning, using playing cards and off-text improvisations (three key components of the Out of Joint rehearsal methodology). It was also important, however, to give the group the experience of researching a topic in a way that replaced the research phase of an Out of Joint verbatim play; interviewing people with specific knowledge and experience of the topic and then replaying that interview back to the rest of the group. This material would then, in a professional context, be given to a writer to sculpt into a script. For the purposes of this exercise, however, we decided on the three key themes yielded by the interview material we had collected and in smaller groups edited the interview transcripts under these subheadings. I then took this material away and edited the final script which we actioned together the following day.

The week was divided into three sections: research Monday and Tuesday, scripting Wednesday and rehearsal Thursday and Friday morning. An informal showing took place on Friday afternoon followed by a debriefing session.

Response

Feedback for the week was very positive. Below are some quotes from emails I received following our week's work together:

Thank you for a really enjoyable workshop. I learnt so much and was quite inspired by the techniques you demonstrated.

I've bought and read *Verbatim* which is a terrific introduction to the various flavours of verbatim work and to the motivations of the original creators – and read *Talking to Terrorists* – and started planning my project with people with dementia as the voiceless that verbatim theatre might be able to empower.

It was a great experience working with you. You created a super-relaxed and open atmosphere amongst a pretty diverse bunch.

Catharine Arakelian

Just a quick note to say thank you so much for last week. The whole week was so much fun and I greatly appreciated your patience and generosity with what you know.

Mark Shields

Thanks a lot for the course. It was excellent.

Chris Sivewright

Great to work with you, it was a really interesting week and really inspiring.

Claire Nelson

www.nickhernbooks.co.uk

 facebook.com/nickhernbooks

 twitter.com/nickhernbooks